The Nature of Texas

Number Eleven: *The Louise Lindsey Merrick Texas Environment Series*

The Nature of Texas

A FEAST OF NATIVE BEAUTY

FROM *Texas Highways* MAGAZINE

Howard Peacock, Editor

FOREWORD BY FRANK LIVELY

TEXAS A&M UNIVERSITY PRESS

 College Station

Frontispiece: May scene between Mason and Llano. The field is blanketed with white sleepy daisy (*Aphanostephys skirrhobasis*), red gaillardia (*Gaillardia amblyodon*), bluebonnet (*Lupinus* sp.), and golden thelesperma (*Thelesperma* sp.). —Bill Reaves

The paper used in this book meets the minimum requirements of the American National Standard for Permanence of Paper for Printed Library Materials, Z39.48-1984. Binding materials have been chosen for durability.

Library of Congress Cataloging-in-Publication Data

The Nature of Texas : a feast of native beauty
    from Texas highways magazine / Howard
    Peacock, editor ; foreword by Frank Lively.
    — 1st ed.
        p. cm. — (The Louise Lindsey
    Merrick Texas environment series ; no. 11)
        ISBN 0-89096-402-5
        1. Natural history—Texas. I. Peacock,
    Howard H., 1925- . II. Texas highways.
    III. Series.
    QH105.T4N38 1990
    508.764—dc20   89-20277
                                            CIP

To Eugenia Porter Rayzor,
whose heart and hand respond to people and nature's own everywhere,
with perhaps a slight favoritism toward those in her beloved Texas.

But ask now the beasts, and they shall teach thee;
    and the fowls of the air, and they shall tell thee:
Or speak to the earth, and it shall teach thee:
    and the fishes of the sea shall declare unto thee.
Who knoweth not in all these that the hand of the Lord
    hath wrought this?
In whose hand is the soul of every living thing,
    and the breath of all mankind.

                                        —JOB 12:7-10

Contents

Foreword

This book might well be called the "The Diversity of Texas." Or "The Beauty of Texas." Or "Unbelievable Texas." Certainly the Lone Star State is all of these.

Some unfortunate souls who have never visited Texas still believe it is a flat, dry country of cowboys, cattle, and cactus. Flat it's not. Elevation ranges from sea level to 8,751 feet, and we have ninety mountains that are more than one mile high. Dry it's not. We have more square miles of inland waterways than any state except Alaska. We have other superlatives: more than six hundred miles of coastline on the Gulf of Mexico; more species of birds counted than in any other state; and more than five thousand species of wildflowers, far more than in any other state. Some have said that about the only thing Texas doesn't have is snow—deep snow for skiing, that is.

For more than fifteen years, *Texas Highways* magazine has been showing and telling the world about our state's great diversity of landscapes, rivers, mountains, forests, flowers, animals, and people, just to mention a few. Judging from the letters from out-of-state readers, they never cease to marvel at the beauty and magnitude of Texas.

Texas Highways' coverage of these subjects got Howard Peacock, a talented writer from East Texas, to thinking, which is tough on a fellow who likes to sit on his back porch and watch the squirrels and listen to the birds. He wrote to us in June, 1987: "I would like to help produce a book on the natural wonders and riches of Texas, using a wise and potent selection of *Texas Highways* stories about wild plants, places, minerals, and creatures." He had selected scores of nature articles "written with excellence and photographed with power" that he wanted to consider. It sounded like a "natural" to us.

We soon had the approval of Texas A&M University Press for a book, so Howard went to work. By the time he had reviewed issues dating back five or six years, narrowing the subjects from about eighty down to book size, editing some articles, writing others, Howard was a little older and wiser.

"I once thought editors had plush and pontifical jobs, mostly looking out the window, saying 'yea yea' or 'nay nay' to writers, averaging about a hundred nays to each yea," says Howard. "It was a shock to learn otherwise. They sweat deadlines, create themes and ideas, fool with writers, and do all sorts of messy tasks, just like regular working folks."

But he believes there is a more important factor: loyalty to the readers. "That's what I've learned to admire most about *Texas Highways* editors," adds Howard. "Their decisions hinge on that sense of loyalty. Maybe it's more than sense. Call it instinct. In editing this book, I've tried to measure up to that high mark."

FRANK LIVELY Editor, *Texas Highways*

Preface

Good nature writing and photography happen everywhere these days, in virtually every corner of the world where nature is given half a chance to survive and express itself. Even in ancient times Job reminded us of what nature can teach. His magnificent passage serves as this book's epigraph.

The chances, however, seem to grow more precious each year, perhaps each passing week. The rolling seas now hurl sprays of poison and plastic. The "lungs of the planet," our rain forests and other deep woods, are ripped by chain-saws so that cattle may graze amid the stumps and produce hamburgers that thicken an already wheezing-fat populace. Once-wild rivers grow rank, cramped by concrete banks. Even the horizons are now layered with mustard-colored murk.

But in those places where nature persists, beauty and knowledge come forth in words and images. And some of the finest nature writing and photography today appear in the pages of *Texas Highways* magazine.

Texas Highways is the bible of Lone Star travelers who love nature's ways and works. The magazine covers more than nature, of course — historical sites, attractions and amusements, native eats, festivals, what have you. That every hotel and motel room in Texas doesn't offer guests the latest issue is an amazing oversight. But nature stories seem to stand apart. Any observant and feeling person from anywhere on the globe who travels Texas roads must sense the immense impact of landforms, plants, and wild creatures on Texas life and character. Indeed, every section of the state has its own peculiar treasures of nature.

The first part of this book portrays a variety of environments in Texas. The second part focuses on some striking inhabitants. Both of these views hark to Job's ancient admonition to learn from the earth and from every living thing in it.

The pity of editing a book like this is being unable to pack all the treasures of plant, animal, mineral, and land lore between two covers. But any book on nature should be merely a prologue, an enticement for further and sharper looking, for more walks in the woods or treks on the beach or leanings against logs.

Most of the articles and pictures here were selected from more than one hundred feature stories on nature that have appeared in *Texas Highways* over the past several years. They were chosen for their own qualities of excellence and for representing various regions of Texas. In a few instances, original material has been written to achieve a balance of coverage.

Every article has been edited to focus on elemental nature, not humanized activity. For the most part, human spoor in these articles has been eliminated or minimized. If that kind of editing offends someone, sorry. But this book is meant to portray nature's special show in just one province of a world that keeps on shrinking, getting more crowded with pushy people, becoming more and more confused with rampant technology and pervasive plastic. "The bottom rung's on the top of the ladder this time," as the saying goes.

Readers of *Texas Highways* will note that these stories appear differently than when the magazine first published them. One reason is the removal of parts of the text and photography that referred strictly to human activity. Another is that a few of the original photographs or color separations are no longer available. The result is a fresh aspect to the stories while retaining the nature-oriented work of the writers and photographers.

If it were not for its state parks, flowered roadsides, and magnificent national parks and preserves, Texas would be much poorer in its legacies. Two giants deserve a word of tribute here: the late Roy Bedichek for his classic book *Adventures with a Texas Naturalist*, and former U.S. Senator Ralph W. Yarborough for leading the fight in Congress year after year to preserve desecrated and disappearing Texas areas of world-class significance. Bedicheck's book opened eyes and hearts to nature's wonders in Texas. Those eyes and hearts would likely be crusted over 'til doomsday without it. Yarborough staked out and fought in the front lines of the 1950s and 1960s for national legislation that established for posterity the Big Thicket National Preserve, Padre Island National Seashore, and Guadalupe Mountains National Park. Any one of those three achievements would amount to a life's work for most people. Remarkable champions of Texas nature, those two.

In this context, I also salute Harold Scarlett, environmental writer for the *Houston Post*. Over the years his fair, fact-filled, comprehensive, cleanly written columns have kept millions of Texans informed of crucial environmental issues. Without question he is among the few great environmental reporters in America.

Help in editing this book came from many points and persons. The *Texas Highways* staff has been superb in its assistance, particularly Jack Lowry's aid and interest. Besides being a solid and imaginative editor, Jack is also a first-rate nature writer and companion in the field. I owe Editor Frank Lively much gratitude, and wish he would shake up a batch of his world-renowned margaritas to help me properly express it.

Special thanks go to Mary-Love Bigony, managing editor of *Texas Parks & Wildlife* magazine, for providing several important photographs from *Texas Parks & Wildlife* files, and to Capital Spectrum Inc. of Austin for duplicating those color separations for this book.

Use of the lovely photographs for "Winged Beauties" by Geyata Ajilvsgi and several other photographs in the book would not have been possible without the problem-solving expertise and understanding of Wallace Engraving Company of Austin. We are grateful.

Most of all, I thank the thousands of Texans and visitors to Texas who not only appreciate nature's bounty and brilliance in these parts, but also do all they can—whatever they can—to protect and extend such loveliness and grace, such richness in form and vibrancy, everywhere.

HOWARD PEACOCK

The Nature of Texas

Strong winds have partially exposed the massive root system of Havard shin oaks in the Monahans sand dunes.—Larry Hodge

A Land for All

ROSEMARY WILLIAMS

Generations ago, when trail-breakers first stood on Texas soil, they gazed at pristine vistas and rough-and-tumble landscapes much like the ones on these pages. The mountains of West Texas captivated and challenged them, as did the awesome desert. Streams and rivers spread out before them, and the overwhelming waters of the Gulf filled their horizon. The pungent Piney Woods of East Texas enthralled and sheltered them, and the panoramas of the Panhandle lured them northward.

Today, you can look upon the same unsullied scenes that once entranced our pioneers. You can view vast areas of Texas that appear unmarked by time and humankind. No wonder. The state encompasses some 275,416 square miles, a space large enough to meet the pressing needs of a progressive society, with lots of elbow room left over.

Texas' vastness gives birth to a geographical gamut. The western sector so little resembles the eastern that the lands seem almost to represent different continents. The spare and mountainous Trans-Pecos symbolizes an alien and exotic region to those who live in the thickly forested realms of East Texas. And similar diversity marks the state's surface elevation, as it rises from sea level on the Gulf to 8,749 feet at the summit of Guadalupe Peak, one of ninety-one Texas mountains a mile or more high.

If you were to walk the 801 straight-line miles north to south across Texas, it would take you about twenty-seven 30-mile days, and you would see terrain that varies from plains to rolling hills to subtropics. You would encounter plant life that ranges from scrub brush to palm trees. And you would seldom go thirsty.

Lakes abound throughout the state. More than five thousand square miles of lakes and streams place Texas second only to Alaska in the amount of inland water. Toledo Bend Reservoir forms the largest reservoir in Texas or on its borders, with approximately 185,000 surface acres. Lake Sam Rayburn is the largest body of water wholly within the state. The Rio Grande, the international boundary between Texas and Mexico, extends 1,248 miles and is the state's longest river, followed by the Red.

Texas' largest county, Brewster, could contain the entire state of Connecticut within its 6,169 square miles, or it could hold about forty-eight counties the size of Rockwall, the state's smallest at 128 square miles.

Texas' huge expanse and variety of terrain collaborate to produce vegetation of unparalleled range and beauty. You can wander through fields of bluebonnets, Indian paintbrush, coreopsis, and hundreds of other multicolored blooms in the spring and watch them give way to the primroses, wood-sorrels, and brown-eyed susans of summer and fall. You can track down the wild azaleas in the east. Or you can stand

A January snowfall in Copper Breaks State Park near Quanah shows the variety of Texas winter scenery.—Wyman Meinzer →

3

Scudding clouds in this scene near Marathon remind hikers how quickly the weather can change during a West Texas autumn.—Jack Lewis

in awe when cactus blooms pepper the western desert with brilliant color after a rare shower.

But today, this moment, you need not travel anywhere. You can visit this

Texas palmettos (Sabal texana), *like these near Mission, are the state's only native treelike palm.*—*Texas Parks and Wildlife Department*

beautiful state, this entrancing Texas, merely by turning these pages. Feast your eyes. And remember. Once, long ago, our forebears reveled in this same splendor.

PART I

Speak to the Earth

Or speak to the earth, and it shall teach thee. . . .
                                        —JOB 12:8

Palo Duro

JACK LOWRY

When you cross the High Plains and discover colorful Palo Duro Canyon spread before you, you feel the wonderment that must have overtaken Indian chieftains and Spanish explorers centuries ago.

If you come on a typical day and ford the small Prairie Dog Town Fork of the Red River, you probably wouldn't believe that this creek sculpted the huge formations around you. But return during a downpour and you will see how quickly the stream becomes a powerful river capable of clawing deep into the land.

The layers of rock at Palo Duro span hundreds of millions of years, but where stream channels are just beginning, geologists say that the canyon is only as old as the last heavy rain.

Even casual observers liken the scene at Palo Duro to the Texas-sized Grand Canyon of the Colorado. The geologic record exposed in the Panhandle Plains is an extension of what visitors would see in Arizona. The age of the rocks in the floor of Palo Duro Canyon is the same as those on the rim of the Grand Canyon. Palo Duro then extends upward six hundred to eight hundred feet

More than 250 million years ago, Permian seas covered what is now the canyon floor, depositing red clay. Evaporation caused layers of white gypsum to be formed throughout the clay.—Randy Green

and involves the last 250 million years of the earth's history.

Historians, too, can draw comparisons between the canyons. In 1541, Francisco Vásquez de Coronado happened upon Palo Duro Canyon during his search for the mythical golden city of Quivira.

But nearly twelve thousand years before the Spaniards ever saw Palo Duro, Indians found shelter, water, and food within the canyon walls. The surrounding grassy plains were jeweled with small lakes where birds, mammoths, and bison watered.

Palo Duro Canyon was named for the junipers that grow on the canyon walls; the Indians fashioned bows and arrows from the juniper's hard wood or *palo duro.*

It was not until 1852 that the first Anglo-American beheld Palo Duro. Captain Randolph B. Marcy was awestruck when he reached the canyon rim in the summer of 1852: "We all . . . stopped and gazed with wonder and admiration upon a panorama which was now for the first time exhibited to the eyes of civilized man. . . . It was as if it had been designed and executed by the almighty artist as the presiding genius of these dismal solitudes."

Marcy likened the formations to the walls of a medieval castle, with battlements and watchtowers standing against the clear blue sky.

Palo Duro Canyon State Park formally opened July 4, 1934. Since then, the 15,743-acre park has grown into one of the state's most popular destinations, attracting half a million visitors per

A cottonwood stands in brilliant contrast to a shadowed bluff in the bottom of Palo Duro Canyon.—Randy Green

year. You enter the park by retracing the footsteps of Comanche chieftain Quanah Parker and of rancher Charles Goodnight, but the descent is also a journey through geologic time.

The oldest exposed rock, on the floor and lower canyon walls, is the Quartermaster Formation of the Permian period, some 230 million to 280 million years old. The formation contains distinctive red shales intermixed with gray shales, clays, mudstones, and sandstones. Large veins of white gypsum also course through it. Above the Quartermaster lies the Tecovas Forma-

tion of the Late Triassic age of 200 million years ago. The rock consists of white, yellow, gray, purplish, and lavender shales and thin layers of soft sandstones. The city of Amarillo (Spanish for "yellow") was named for Amarillo Creek, where the yellow bed of the Tecovas formation crops out miles from the canyon.

Whereas the Quartermaster is made of marine deposits, the rocks of the Tecovas are formed from sediments deposited in swamps and streams. Among the fossils found are those of an extinct crocodiloid reptile known as the phyto-

saur, and lung-fish teeth.

A giant amphibian called *Metoposaurus* also lived here. The animal resembled a seven-foot-long salamander. It submerged itself in the bottom of a swamp and waited for fish to pass. A third eye allowed it to direct its gaping mouth to its prey.

Beaver, some two hundred species of birds, including residents and migrants, and the elusive mule deer are among the dwellers of this rugged region in the present age.

Trails take you to some of the canyon's best-known features. You can mount up and spend hours exploring fifteen hundred acres of canyon land on horseback. Or the Sad Monkey Railroad tour, which runs regularly in good weather, offers a quick overview of area biology, lore, and geology in this immense sculpture of earth and rock created by the Prairie Dog Town Fork.

The Prairie Dog Town Fork of the Red River flows through the park past shimmering cottonwoods and red canyon walls. Tough junipers that gave Palo Duro Canyon its name thrive in higher elevations. —Jack Lewis

The Lighthouse rises nearly three hundred feet from the canyon floor. This distinctive formation is one of the most widely recognized features in the canyon.—Jack Lewis →

Our Vanishing Prairies

Story and photographs by
JIM BONES

Around the world, light fills prairie grasses with life, while chlorophyll makes sweet sugars from lean air, water, and sunshine. Every day, bright plains hum with the industry of thin green blades that breathe carbon dioxide and exhale fresh oxygen for the benefit of all creatures.

When the United States was still young and settlers moved west, more than half of North America supported native grasslands. In 1845, Texas entered the Union as the largest prairie state. Now, virtually nothing remains of the original savannas, prairies, and plains of Texas.

History could be told from the viewpoint of the grasses and associated wild plants and animals that make up the oldest natural heritage of Texas. The tragic story might unfold from dim beginnings in the geologic past, through the boom and bust of the cattle and cowboy era, and the beat-down, worn-out soil of today's farmlands and urban sprawl. If we do not make a stand for the turf today, the story might also foretell a desolate future that drifts

Little bluestem (tall rusty grass), King Ranch bluestem (fine tan in the foreground), panic grass (green broadbladed grass in left foreground in front of phlox), and Virginia bluestem (tall clumps) thrive on post oak savannahs invaded by mesquite. →

Sideoats grama, the state grass of Texas, provides high-quality forage in summer and winter.

Flooded grasses stand by a lake margin in an East Texas forest.

ahead like the dust storms of the past.

Grass is tough and old, much more than you and I. Its ancestors lived with the dinosaurs. It fed huge herds of prehistoric creatures and outlasted the mighty millions of bison that darkened the vast plains.

Between five and ten thousand years ago, the domestication of grass with grains first made civilizations possible. Stone Age hunters lived in Texas then. They followed and fed on now extinct grazers.

The settlements of sixteenth-century European immigrants brought destruction to the Indians and the land. In less than four hundred years, the forests were cut down, the ranges grazed to dirt. Finally, for profit or for subsistence, the sod was busted and forever turned under. As farmers plowed the land and ranchers allowed it to be overgrazed, the true riches of the topsoil slowly wasted away.

Despite their antiquity, many native grasslands may not last to the end of this century. Agricultural, industrial, and domestic development continue to threaten premature extinction. In Texas alone, the once long grass prairie has been reduced to about two thousand acres of hay land.

J. O. Langford, a West Texas homesteader, recounted first-hand the changes that swept West Texas grasslands over the first three decades of the twentieth century (in *Big Bend: A Homesteader's Story*, by J. O. Langford with Fred Gipson [Austin: University of Texas Press, 1952]). In 1909 he and his family found grasses in abundance in the Big Bend area:

As the sun climbed higher, the green grassed slopes began to shimmer in the heat. Never have I seen such grass as grew in West Texas in those days. Endless miles of it stretched out in every direction. It stood knee-deep to a horse everywhere, and wherever there was room for a grass plant to grow, there one grew. Clear up to the tops of the highest ridges it grew, almost hiding the glistening rim-rocks; and down on the slopes and in the valleys, only the tallest of the desert plants stood out above it.

Border raids during the Mexican Revolution forced the Langfords to leave the Big Bend for El Paso. When they returned less than two decades later, the landscape had changed:

And now, where once I'd thought there was more grass than could ever be eaten off, I found no grass at all. Just the bare, rain-eroded ground. . . .
We came back in 1927. We built a store and established the Hot Springs Post Office. We built tourist courts for the convenience of customers, who, with the aid of automobiles and improved roads, came to the spring in ever-increasing numbers. We stayed there until 1942. . . . I suppose we could say that we prospered.

Yet, never again did we have that which we'd had in the beginning. Somehow, the brightness seemed gone from the land.

If the genetic wealth of wild grasses vanishes, we will lose our source of new hybrid grains. The result could be the wholesale impoverishment of humanity. This is the sober legacy we inherit today. But we are also left with wisdom about the way we are shaped as we mold the earth with our hands.

The Clymer Blackland Prairie, along with the Meador Prairie and the Smiley Meadow, all in North Texas — three patches of grassland, twenty-five hundred acres in all, represent the largest expanses of unbroken, ungrazed native sod left in the state.

The loss of native grasslands may not seem as important or exciting as news about world terror, but even that will seem insignificant if the genetic variability of the past meets with extinction. We should remember the wild places that have been sacrificed and encourage the preservation of the wild places that remain.

Caddo Lake

TRACY OWENS TORMA

You can hear the quiet and feel the stillness in the air.

The Caddo Indians must have felt the same hushed presence after the great storm pounded their northeast Texas tribal lands with rain and left behind an eerie body of water, a maze of shallow channels and bayous filled with gnarled cypress trees and mossy swamps.

That same peaceful stillness still draws visitors to Caddo Lake State Park on the upper end of one of the South's largest natural lakes in the Piney Woods of Northeast Texas. Some believe the lake was formed by the New Madrid earthquake, which shook all the southern states in 1811, caused the current of the Mississippi River to reverse momentarily, and also created Reelfoot Lake in Tennessee.

Spanish explorers of the sixteenth century were probably the first white men to view this mysterious watery environment. Then it was a chain of small lakes and winding bayous known as Laguna Espanola.

According to Caddo Indian legend, in a dream the Great Spirit warned an important chieftain of impending danger. The chief moved his tribe to higher ground in time to escape the heavy

Evening sunlight settles on Spanish-moss-covered cypress at Caddo Lake.—Randy Green

rains that filled a gap in the trembling earth and formed Caddo Lake.

While the Caddo Indian legend is romantic and the New Madrid earthquake theory exciting, a more plausible explanation is that a series of natural logjams known as the Great Raft blocked the Red River and forced water back into its tributaries to form the lake.

Today, the lake's natural beauty beckons visitors to the area and the state park, with its 478 acres lying next to historic Big Cypress Bayou in a primeval wooded setting. Tall loblolly and shortleaf pines, mixed with oaks, hickories, and other hardwoods, plus an abundance of other native plants and flowers and wildlife make the park a nature lover's haven.

Campers who want to become familiar with their surroundings should make a stop at the visitor center, which has displays on wildlife and vegetation in the area. The rustic stone center also offer exhibits and information about Caddo Lake and its history. A leaflet furnished for identifying trees enables visitors to study nature along several miles of hiking trails.

Bird watchers can glimpse both native and migratory birds, including the bobwhite, wood duck, barred owl, ruby-throated hummingbird, green heron, great blue heron, and red-shouldered hawk.

Caddo Lake's eerie beauty also lures

Lily pads often grow at the base of cypress trees.— Randy Green

Misty mornings such as this one are ideal times to walk the shoreline.— Randy Green

photographers, who roam the channels and bayous seeking to capture the swamplike scenery with their lenses. Visitors with patience and relative still-ness come away with the best memories and pictures of deer, raccoon, opossum, fox, and other animals of the wet woods.

Big Thicket: Mystical Microcosm

HOWARD PEACOCK

"Oh yeah," said Bill Brett, tipping on the back legs of his kitchen chair, "there's a mystique about the Big Thicket. I know it. I've felt it. So have plenty of others."

He was talking to a TV interviewer at his spread near Hull. Facing the cameras, they were discussing why Brett, a world-class storyteller and writer of short stories, had spent his sixty-plus years in the Big Thicket of southeast Texas. Was there a mystique about the place? How would he describe it?

"You might say it's the mixture," Brett reflected. "A lot of pure nature and a lot of human nature, all th'owed together."

Today's mystique centers around the Thicket's wild orchids, meat-eating plants, lush ferns, rare birds, and a science-stunning confluence of eight major ecological systems. "America's Ark," one writer nicknamed the Big Thicket. "The Biological Crossroads of North America," corrected another, amazed at a profusion of life forms ranging from alligators to zygospores.

The Big Thicket once covered 3.5 million acres of wilderness. Then came towns, farms, ranches, highways, lumber industries, oil booms, second-home developments, and other forms of "progress." Less than one-tenth of the primitive Big Thicket remains today, and parts of that fragment disappear weekly.

The single note of salvation is the Big Thicket National Preserve and a few private land gifts. A fifty-year fight to save parts of the Big Thicket for posterity, waged largely between conservationists and some commercial interests, ended October 11, 1974, in a compromise. Pres. Gerald Ford signed a bill authored by U.S. Representative Charles Wilson of Lufkin that created America's first National Preserve of 84,550 acres.

Even with all the cutting and developing, no other area of comparable size on the continent or perhaps on the entire globe can match the Big Thicket for natural diversity. Even the United Nations recognizes this fact, naming the Thicket as one of the rare places in the world qualifying for the UN's Man and the Biosphere Program. This ongoing project studies the changes taking place in the earth's natural systems.

For most visitors to the Thicket, it is enough to know that the region contains two of the few stretches of wild river remaining in Texas, environments from sand-dune desert to Okeefenokee-type swamp to Appalachian-type uplands, silent woodland "cathedrals," and trees — millions upon millions of trees, of all sizes and most kinds.

Huge trees like the American beech, maples, oaks, and sky-punching pines. Middlin' trees like black cherry, hophornbeam, ironwood, and sassafras. Small trees like the dogwood, grancy-graybeard, tingle-tongue, and farkle-berry. Tiny trees like club moss. Club moss used to grow as tall as a loblolly pine grows now, but those were pre-

Carnivorous yellow pitcher plants (Sarracenia alata) *thrive in high-acidity bogs in the Big Thicket.—John Tveten*

Fungi such as this (Leucocoprinus fragilissimus) *thrive in the moist lands of the Thicket, providing clumps of stunning ground cover.—John Tveten*

historic epochs. Today, you measure club moss with a four-inch ruler.

All told, the Big Thicket contains close to two hundred species of trees and wild shrubs. Some are natives of the tropics, some occur naturally as far north as Newfoundland. Others thrive at points between these extremes. In the Big Thicket, they have been gathered together and bunched up.

The most famous tree in the Thicket grew near the place where three counties—Polk, Hardin, and Tyler—come together. An unknown pioneer named it "the Witness Tree" because its massive trunk and outreaching limbs had shaded secret Indian ceremonies. La-Salle's explorers passed beneath it in the seventeenth century. Many settlers had shaken hands there to seal property agreements. When it was killed, the tree was probably some one thousand years old—a grandiose age for a Southern magnolia. In 1966, Lance Rosier, a self-taught naturalist who was once described as the "St. Francis of the Big Thicket," guided U.S. Supreme Court Justice William O. Douglas through hummocky woods to view this former giant. By then it had crumbled to a whitened trunk. Rosier showed Douglas five holes that had been bored into the trunk. Through them, the killers had poured arsenate of lead into the cambium layer, the tree's circulatory sapworks, just under the bark.

Douglas was aghast.

"Why?" he groaned, his voice cracking in disgust and anger.

"To scare people," Rosier replied. "To discourage people from trying to save

parts of the Thicket for a national park."

That might have been the day that the fortunes of the Big Thicket turned around.

Any season is a good season to visit the Thicket, but springtime is the showiest. The parade of a thousand kinds of flowers begins in February. First come crimson clusters along the bare branches of the maple trees, then redbuds and dogwoods, wild azaleas, and some species of wild orchids. Then, grancy-graybeards and more wild orchids and sylvan ferns.

Springtime surprises in the Thicket include the blooming of four of North America's five genera of meat-eating plants. Pitcher plants produce a big buttery yellow flower with maroon seeds. These oddities lure insects, and sometimes small frogs, into long, hooded tubes, with hundreds of down-turning hairs that fight back all attempts by the victims to escape. Pink-flowered sundews and blue butterworts trap ants and other prey on sticky leaves, then roll them up like enchiladas. The wiliest of the meat-eaters, the bladderwort, springs underwater trap-doors on unsuspecting bugs swimming in the dark, acidic ponds these plants favor. Masses of small golden flowers held aloft on six pontoons betray the bladderwort's presence.

Summertime has its own flowers, notably various species of coreopsis and coneflowers, but also certain wild orchids that like humid heat. Bugs and insects come forth to feast on the new leaves that clothe the Thicket. Leaves

Luxuriant growth around an acidic bog in the traditional "Bear Hunters' Thicket" typifies the tremendous diversity of species of trees and other plant life found in the Big Thicket.— Howard Peacock

are often works of art in themselves and worth study. In turn, many of the region's 350 species of resident and migrant birds appear early and late in the season to feast on the bugs that feast on the leaves.

Summer's the season to watch multitudes of baby critters born in the springtime learning the ways of the wild. It is also the time for river-swimming or bathing in a shady creek. On late afternoons, the top of the water is warm from the day's sun, almost like a sitz bath. One's body oozes apart. Feet and ankles, however, chill instantly when they hit pockets of cold water that have settled in the sand or stir up small icy currents moving along the bottoms. The contrast startles flesh and bones alike.

Fall brings color to two dozen species of the Thicket's trees, shrubs, and vines. Sugar maples, beeches, shoe-peg maples, sassafras, hickories, tupelos, sweetgums, and various oaks are a few of the species of trees and wild shrubs that canopy the Thicket in patches and panoramas of fall brilliance.

Winter brings clear, cool days and long views to the Thicket. Hardwoods have shed their leaves and stand in naked silhouette, their framework revealing miracles of nature's engineers. Woods once dense now open up. Where the view in the summer could pierce only a few feet ahead, it stretches for a hundred yards in the winter. One can walk ten times more in the winter air, which photographers and artists say at times rivals the clarity of the air in rural

Greece or the mountains of Santa Fe. If snow falls, which occurs in the upper Thicket every two or three years, the majesty of the deep woods heightens. Winter's forest floor is a mosaic of fallen leaves, spongy to the step and laced with muted hues. And against a deep blue winter sky, the evergreens of the Thicket shine and glint greener than ever.

If there exists a bona fide "Big Thicket mystique," of the kind Bill Brett and others have known, you are apt to find it among a grove of trees deep in the wild. That is where it hit the most eloquent and forceful of modern Thicket spokesmen, the late Archer Fullingim, who for twenty-five years, as editor of the weekly *Kountze News*, championed the Big Thicket against any and all who would destroy or desecrate it.

In a column written in 1972, he coined a phrase, "the Holy Ghost Thicket." He confessed to his readers, "In the depths of the Thicket in Pine Island Bayou and Black Creek watershed, I get the Holy Ghost and talk in tongues. I had never talked in tongues before. . . ." He told of a green canopy of leaves with slivers of sunlight sifting through to the East Texas earth and ended with a prophecy: "The grandchildren of the young will be glad to flee to the depths of the Thicket in their days after 2000 A.D."

Though the rest of the countryside be leveled and covered over with pavement, the wilderness and mystique of the Big Thicket will endure.

Where Bayou Meets the Bay

BARBARA HINTON

Cool breezes rush through dark piney woods on their way to rustle prairie grasses. Forest creatures drink from streams that flow into the breeding ground of salt water shrimp. Canoeists paddle in quiet waters not far from monuments to computer-quiet technology. Strange contrasts? They come with the territory at Armand Bayou Park and Nature Center.

With seventeen hundred acres preserved in a wilderness state, the Armand Bayou Park offers a wide spectrum of recreational and educational opportunities. Only thirty minutes from downtown Houston and about the same distance from Galveston, the park provides a wondrous escape from urban living.

As one of the last coastal waterways that remains almost intact, the bayou mixes here with salt water from the bay to create a brackish home for shrimp, crabs, a variety of fish, and other marine organisms. The intricate relationship between East Texas forest, Gulf Coast prairie, and Galveston Bay marshes also supports a diverse community of land animals, including deer, armadillos, coyotes, and raccoons. Marshes offer feeding and breeding grounds for herons and ducks, while prairie and woods house hawks and

Morning mists shroud the rising sun over the peaceful bayou.—Jack Lewis

Salt marsh mallow resembles hibiscus.
—Jack Lewis

An elaborate marine life display shows the bayou as a complete estuarine system.

Outside, nature tours introduce visitors to Armand Bayou. Guided hikes and self-guided tours offer many different trails for exploration. The Karankawa and Jimmy Martyn trails lead through piney woods to marshland and the bayou. The Prairie Trail explores the coastal prairie, which is being restored to native wilderness condition. The Jimmy Martyn Trail also takes the visitor to the Indian village. For seven thousand years, hunting along the banks and canoeing the waters, the Karankawa, Attacapa, and Coahuiltecan tribes lived off these lands. Guides tell of Indian lore and legends. Classes teach almost forgotten skills—how to build willow branch and palmetto huts, shape clay into pottery, weave grasses into mats.

Nature Center expeditions also recapture early life-styles. Night hikes and bird classes explore the multitude of species native to the region. Water investigations and seining reveal an unusual variety of aquatic communities. Wildflower identification and classes in landscaping with native plants teach naturalists of all ages the wonders of these surroundings.

The preserve's nearness to a giant metroplex creates an additional opportunity to monitor and evaluate the changes caused by today's congested population centers. Climatic conditions at Armand Bayou differ markedly from those in the nearby urban areas. The temperature in warm weather is

owls. Transition zones support turtles, lizards, salamanders, and frogs. Vegetation is equally diverse, with saltgrasses and bluestem grass; hickories, oaks, and elms; small stands of magnolia; and an understory of palmetto and vines.

A shaded path leads from the parking area to the preserve. Honeysuckle and grapevines form a bridge overhead. In a broad clearing appears a gray, barn-like building with wide porches, open doors, and huge windows. Approaching this interpretive center, the visitor discovers a macrame spider web suspended in midair. Then inside, spilled out on a table like the contents from dozens of little boys' pockets, are bones and antlers, fur and feathers, wasp nests and turtle shells—treasures from countless childhood explorations. The sign on a wooden box says, "Look inside at the world's most dangerous animal"; a mirror reflects the looker's own image.

often fifteen to twenty degrees cooler in the park than in the city, forty to fifty degrees cooler than on the traffic-jammed Gulf Freeway. The preserve receives more rainfall annually than nearby Houston, yet it comes in a gentle fashion with less chance of flooding and destruction. A tall upper story of trees, a second story of shrubs and smaller plants, and an understory of ground cover and grasses help cleanse the air of pollutants and prevent the quick evaporation of moisture.

With its endless breezes, its timeless wilderness, its birds and animals living as nature planned, Armand Bayou remains a natural treasure to be studied and enjoyed, revealing its wonders to all those who wish to discover them.

From a limb low over the water, an American egret breaks the still surface of the bayou as it snares breakfast.—Jack Lewis

Guadalupe Trails

Story and photographs by
RANDY GREEN

From the east, the Guadalupe Mountains loom above the horizon like the dark ragged clouds of an approaching norther. Forty-niners heading for the California gold fields watched the sun set behind the escarpment for days while they heaved, pushed, and cursed their teams across the tortured land of sand dunes and arroyos west of the Pecos River and on toward the rugged ridges.

Arrival at the base of the mountains was worth the trials of the journey. Cool pine forests and abundant springs awaited, offering travelers a chance to recuperate before they continued on across the searing salt flats to El Paso.

The great towering ridges in the Guadalupe Mountains National Park are composed of Permian reef limestone. They mark the edges of the largest exposed slice of such reef in the world. During the Permian age, about 230 million to 280 million years ago, a large shallow sea covered much of what is now West Texas. Lime-secreting algae and reef-building animals such as sponges and brachiopods grew in profusion along the edges of the sea. The limestone gradually built up, aided by the rise and fall of sea level during the period.

Eventually, the sea retreated for the last time. About ten million years ago, the area around the Guadalupe Mountains and the Sierra Diablo rose and tilted, exposing great, massive cliffs and walls of the ancient reef towering thousands of feet above the surrounding countryside.

The rugged landscape plays an important role in the area's climate and biology. Prevailing westerly winds slam into the western escarpment, frequently plaguing Guadalupe Pass with prolonged periods of howling winds more than eighty miles per hour. The rising air cools and drops about twice as much precipitation in the mountains—more than twenty inches—as on the lowlands.

The disparity of rainfall and other variables, such as soil depth and protection from the wind, contribute strongly to the wide range of plant communities found within the park. On the lower eastern slopes near the park headquarters and the Pine Springs campground, plants and animals of the Chihuahuan Desert flourish: yucca, sotol, agave, and many species of cacti. Junipers and piñon pine dot the mid-slopes at the foot of the mountains. Oaks and maples grow in protected canyons like McKittrick and by the banks of watercourses like Smith Springs. Above seven thousand feet, sturdy specimens of ponderosa pine, limber pine, and Douglas fir cover the highlands. These conifers grow especially thick in the area called the Bowl, a rugged daylong hike from the Pine Springs campground.

Many of the animals found in the Edwards Plateau to the east and the Chihuahuan Desert to the south can also be found in the Guadalupes. Mule

deer are abundant, as are jackrabbits, ring-tailed cats, gray foxes, porcupines, bobcats, and skunks, especially in the canyons near water. Black bears, once numerous throughout Texas but rapidly killed off by settlers, occasionally can be glimpsed in the high country. The mountains also support a population of cougars.

The park offers surprises for wildlife observers. Ranchers reintroduced elk after native Merriam elk were elimi-

An old alligator juniper grows from the cliffside near Government Spring. Tough, gridlike bark gives the tree its name. Various birds feed on the fruit.

Late afternoon sun brightens bluffs below Hunter Peak. →

A Texas madrone grows by the entrance to North McKittrick Canyon. Smooth pink or white bark makes the tree easy to identify.

nated in the nineteenth century. Herds can be found both on the eastern lowland slopes and in the conifer forests of the highlands. While no species of fish is native to the Guadalupes, rainbow trout and bluegill were successfully established in McKittrick Creek. Birdwatchers can find Stellar's jay in the pine-fir forest of the uplands.

In a sense, things have not changed much for the Guadalupes. Only a comparative handful of Indians, scouts, soldiers, settlers, and visitors have ever witnessed the incomparable beauty of evening light on the massive rock faces or experienced the solitude of the high country.

Ponderosa pines fill the "Bowl" north of Hunter Peak, formerly known as Pine Top.

Longspur columbine (Aquilegia longissima) prefers wet soil. The flower can be found at a few springs in the Big Bend region. — Harry Gordon

Springs of Big Bend

JACK LOWRY

Water — a resource we take for granted, until it becomes scarce. Without water, the land dries up, animals and plants disappear, and soon only blowing sands exist, as in northern Chile's Atacama Desert, where a centimeter of rain in a year is cause for celebration.

In the arid lands of the earth, water is ephemeral, like a ghostly desert spirit that vanishes as quickly as it appears. In East Texas, water is common except in unexpected drought years. In Big Bend National Park, you relish every drop.

Here, nobody takes water for granted. The lifeblood of the desert may not always taste good as it burbles from the ground, but you drink it with gratitude. You know that without this bit of desert magic, the plants and animals would perish.

The desert of Big Bend abounds with brilliant sunlight and fresh air. Only the availability of water places limitations on plant and animal life. Desert flora and fauna must use water efficiently.

Former chief park naturalist Frank Deckert says that all of Big Bend's sixty-plus cactus species have evolved to survive and thrive in the desert. The spines that surround a cactus protect the plant from being eaten, reduce the amount of water loss, and "hold an envelope of air around the plant that protects it from drying winds." The thick cactus stem reduces surface area where moisture might be lost, and the plant's waxy coating seals in water. The plant's root system is shallow and wide-spreading, which allows it to draw up rainwater as it enters the ground.

San Antonio botanist Del Weniger says that the most extreme desert forms of cacti release up to six thousand times less water than an ordinary plant of the same weight. Now, that's adaptation.

Other plants of Big Bend have also adapted to the harsh environment. Ocotillos, which protect themselves with heavy spines, are leafless except around the rainy season. That way they cut down on their need for water.

The prolific creosote bush has a taproot that reaches down thirty feet to find groundwater. A light-reflecting coat of resin protects the plant from moisture loss. Creosote-bush roots produce toxins that discourage competition from other plants.

Big Bend National Park's first superintendent, geologist Ross A. Maxwell, pointed out that one of the best ways to locate water is to watch the doves. When you see them flying in the same direction, they will generally lead you to a spring or tinaja (a cavity in bedrock in which water accumulates).

Game trails, especially well-trodden ones, also lead to water. Direction is the key. You can be sure that deer and bobcats take the quickest route to water. And where you see an unusual abundance of vegetation, you know you are at a water source. "You never know what you're going to run across, a seep or a sparkling stream," Big Bend photographer Earl Nottingham says.

"Most seeps are in the rocks or ground, many surrounded by undergrowth. When you inspect further, you notice things *around* the springs—rock formations, plant life, signs left by animals that depended on that spring for their existence. More than oases, I like to think of Big Bend springs as sanctuaries."

The park contains at least two hundred springs that range from several millimeters of standing water to large pools and flowing streams. Because springs depend ultimately on rainfall to replenish their supply of water, the amount of water at the springs varies seasonally and from year to year. Evaporation rates and the types of vegetation found around the springs also affect their volume of water.

Salt-cedars (tamarisks), for example, were brought from the Mediterranean to Texas for use as a windbreak, for erosion control, and as ornamentals. But the rapidly spreading tree is the bane of arid lands, where it crowds out other vegetation.

Today, it grows wild from California to Florida, doing well wherever it finds a little moisture and sun. The tamarisk has a high tolerance for saline and alkaline soils. In areas of Big Bend park, the tree's insatiable thirst has depleted springs and lowered the water table.

But aside from a few pesky plants, the real danger to the springs comes from humans. The springs form part of the fragile desert ecosystem. You may visit here only briefly, but the things you do will have an impact long after you are gone.

The tiny mesa greggia (Nerisyrenia camporum) *is dwarfed by a lechuguilla, one of the dominant plants of the Chihuahuan Desert.—Bob Parvin*

In arid lands, decay is retarded and a thoughtless camper's litter becomes an unsightly addition to the landscape. Desert springs and streams sustain amphibians, birds, fish, insects, and mammals. If you use soap or other substances, you pollute their precious water.

Nature has reclaimed the area of historic Glenn Spring, where Comanches camped on raids into Mexico, the first Anglo settler in the area grazed horses, and a wax factory once thrived. The spring now pours forth its precious liquid, the desert winds moan as they did long years ago, and wildlife comes to drink. As elsewhere in the park, collecting historic and prehistoric artifacts is strictly prohibited.

One big tinaja is now called Ernst Tinaja. The twenty-by-thirty-foot tinaja is carved by water into the massive limestone creek bed. Off-white, yellowish, gray, and ruddy rock cliffs that have been broken and tilted by faulting rise above the pool. The tinaja holds water year-round.

A series of hot springs occurs along the Rio Grande in the southeast part of the park. The water temperature is 105 degrees year round. Fifty years ago it spewed out a quarter of a million gallons of water per day. Since then, the flow has decreased. Some scientists believe the hot water comes from a reservoir that was deposited at least twenty thousand years ago and is not being replenished. The springs are said to be heated by buried igneous rocks that are still hot.

An old brochure of these hot springs claimed that "sufferers from asthma, kidney diseases, dropsy, jaundice, pellagra, eczema, rheumatism of all forms, stomach troubles including ulcers, tobacco poisoning, hiccough, boils, skin diseases, influenza, sunburn, and genito-urinary diseases have left their troubles here and gone home rejoicing."

After a long day of trekking in Big Bend park under the bright West Texas sun, what could be more refreshing than a dip in the warm springs? "There's nothing better than sitting in the hot springs under a full moon," avows Earl Nottingham.

But the hot springs are not the only ones with regenerative powers. Each watering hole nurtures in its own way, drawing thirsty animals to be healed with a refreshing bit of liquid magic.

A strawberry pitaya cactus blooms on a hillside in Big Bend National Park. The Chisos Mountains appear in the distance.
—Steve Alvarez

In the lower elevations, desert marigold (Baileya multiradiata) appears early in the spring. Tuff (volcanic ash) formations rise in the background near Castolon.
—Randy Green →

Rio Grande

HOWARD PEACOCK

For almost a thousand miles the Rio Grande defines the border between Texas and Mexico. Rising in the San Juan peaks of Colorado at the Continental Divide, the snow-fed torrent drops 12,000 feet to sea level at the Gulf of Mexico. In Texas alone, the waters fall from an altitude of 3,762 feet at El Paso to 15 feet at Port Isabel. Canyons are carved by the river in the Diablo Mountains and the Trans-Pecos country, then its waters, bolstered by the Rio Concho from Mexico, trickle through desert and finally emerge into a meandering waterway of the Coastal Plains. Little wonder that its plants and wildlife range from thin-air breathers of the heights to creatures of the humid tropics.

Along the route of the Rio Grande, the growing season increases from 245 days in the north to 320 days. Longest river in Texas, it is the fourth or fifth longest in the United States, a matter still in dispute.

Myriad species of birds, mammals, reptiles, insects, fishes, and other parts of nature's cornucopia span the river's spectrum from the Big Bend National Park (708,221 acres) in the Chisos Mountains to the Santa Ana National Wildlife Refuge (about 2,000 acres) in the palm-pillared Lower Valley. Big Bend is the one place in the United States to see the Colima warbler; the Lower Valley is the only place in this nation to find green jays, white-fronted doves, and chachalacas in the wild. Assorted other residents of the river's course include antelope, badger, beaver, ocelot, jaguarundi, puma, margay, bobcat, coati, chipmunk, mule deer, javelina, the big-eared desert fox, and, if reported sightings are correct, the yellow-haired porcupine. The range of plant life along the river is prodigious, from minuscule desert thorn to royal palm.

Devil's River and the Pecos are the Rio Grande's main tributaries in Texas, where it drains more than forty thousand square miles.

Bound up with violent human history for ten thousand years, the river has been given names that reflect its character: Río Bravo, Río Turbio, Río de las Palmas, Río San Buenaventura. It was first called Rio Grande in 1598 when Juan de Oñate took possession of the American Northwest in the name of the Spanish king.

High above the Rio Grande in Presidio County, prickly pear blooms glow in a spring sunset.—Richard Reynolds, Texas Dept. of Commerce →

A cougar drinks from the Rio Grande near Langtry after feasting on a kill.—Randy Green →

Near the Gulf of Mexico, palm trees grow along the Rio Grande.—Steve Bentsen

Below Falcon Dam, the Rio Grande meanders along a scenic route towards the Gulf of Mexico.—Randy Green
←

Enchanted Rock

IRA KENNEDY

In the heartland of Texas the pink granite dome of Enchanted Rock rises above the surrounding oak savanna like a megalithic monument. Over the ages the rock has inspired a special reverence in those who allowed their lives to be shaped by its enigmatic presence.

Composed of some of the oldest rock on earth, this ancient landmark began taking shape more than a billion years ago. From the earth's core, underground rivers of molten lava rose like mushrooms that cooled into rock before they surfaced. Cataclysmic changes occurred. Great mountains and oceans rose and fell. Volcanoes thrust skyward; rampaging storms deluged the land.

Bit by bit, erosion worked its way down to the old rock. Finally, some 600 million years ago, Enchanted Rock emerged, eventually to stand 450 feet from base to summit and a square mile in area.

For more than ten thousand years, Enchanted Rock drew Indians to its summit. They held the earth holy and believed its power crystallized as a spirit within the mountains. "Gahe" to the Kiowas, "Gan" to the Apaches, the mountain spirit lived in the caves. According to the Apaches, the Giver of Life sent Gan with the message of a better way to live.

The Comanche believed no less. The vision quest stood at the heart of their culture. From the summit of holy mountains they sought the guidance of the Great Spirit for their life's path.

More than a century ago, most Indian tribes abruptly disappeared from Texas. Trails of tears like molten lava ran toward Indian Territory in Oklahoma. But a few Indians, like my great-grandmother, passed for white rather than move to a distant reservation in a place without ancestors.

Born between two worlds, my grandmother, Rosa Daniels, found the transition from Indian to migrant life a small step that did not go unnoticed. Hers was not a migration from place to place. It was a journey from one culture to another.

Several summers ago, Grandma and I spent a weekend camped at Enchanted Rock. Intermittently over the years she had passed on to me her knowledge of native plants and their uses, but my cursory interest in the subject threatened her efforts until she neared the end of life. Belatedly, I realized the topic held the central place to everything Indian that Grandma instilled in me. Her knowledge of plants endured her cultural changes because, for many years, the survival of her family depended on what she knew. One of my motives for the camping trip was to draw out of Grandma as much as I could on the subject.

After Grandma and I returned to our campsite from a trip to the summit of Enchanted Rock, we sat in the old campgrounds along Sandy Creek and drank iced tea. She told me how her ancestors used the plants that grew in this area and then talked about happenings on the rock in the old days.

"Come to think of it, I've spent the better part of my life within a hundred miles of this place," she said. "All I ever wanted has been right around here, and it was the same with my folks."

The first evening, sitting by the campfire, I asked Grandma to tell me what she knew about Enchanted Rock. She sat in silence for a time. The firelight cast a glow on her tanned and wrinkled skin. And with the shawl wrapped around her shoulders, she looked like someone in an Edward Curtis photograph.

"Listen," she began, "there was a time when this was a holy mountain. The old magic is still here. That'll never change. The white folks tell stories aplenty about this place and how it

come by its name. Ain't all of them goin' to be the actual truth. But this is. What I know come from my folks. Ain't written down nowheres that I know of. But I learned it from them. This ain't just my voice you're hearin'. It's all of them rolled up into one."

"Momma grew up amongst the Comanche, Kiowa, Apache, Delaware, Shawnee, and others. They was all bunched up back then lookin' for a place to live. And ever'body was speakin' different tongues like at the Tower of Babel in the Bible. 'Cept the Indi'ns knew signs. They could talk with their hands and say what they had a mind to.

"Enchanted Rock means Holy Mountain. Like I said, the Indi'ns all

Time and the elements have shaped a garden of stone formations. In the foreground, streaks formed by water runoff can be seen. Legend calls them trails of molten silver tears.—Jack Lewis

Clouds loom over the pinkish-gray surface of Enchanted Rock.—Jack Lewis →

Enchanted Rock   49

crowded in on each other talkin' sign. They named the Rock and called it holy. The sign for sacred rock, holy mountain, and big rock is pretty much the same. There's no sign for enchanted."

As she said each set of words, she spoke in sign. Each gesture flowed into the next with the grace of dance.

"You'll hear stories about the Rock and maybe the folks tellin' 'em hold 'em up as true. I don't know. Some say its name comes from the crackin' sounds heard at night when it's coolin'. Can't say I can speak on that. I never heard such. No. But they's nothin' much in nature could fool the Indi'ns. We lived all in these parts." Her ancient hand brushed across the dark horizon like someone in command of the clouds. "There's the hollow sounds that they talk about. Say it spooked the Indi'ns. But that ain't so. There's a rock right out back sounds like that. The top part is buckled up is all.

"And there's other stories that could stand a new light. Like the one that held the Indi'ns feared the Rock, that they wouldn't even shoot arrows in its direction." Grandma smiled at the notion.

"You'll hear talk, too, of devil spirits and Indi'ns killin' their own on top of the Rock. What some folks won't do to scare up a story! Momma knew all the tribes in these parts, and none of 'em held such notions. None of 'em. They lost more of their kind to war and disease than they could spare. And that's a fact."

Grandma Rosa died four years later.

Over the years, it seemed I would never meet another person whose respect for Enchanted Rock could rival hers. Then I met Warren Watson, the superintendent of Enchanted Rock State Natural Area.

Not long ago, Warren and I sat in his office discussing the rock and its status as a natural area.

"In 1978 the Nature Conservancy bought Enchanted Rock," he began. "There was a real strong interest on their part to protect the rock. They were afraid developers were going to buy it and carve it up. There are, of course, plenty of quarries doing that right now. The conservancy held it until the Parks Department could come up with the money.

"There are so many things to protect here. This is not only a national natural landmark, but we also have certain species of plants that need to be protected. There are archeological sites here, and some of them are on the National Registry of Archeological Sites."

Plants like King Ranch bluestem and Johnson grass are kept out of the area because they encroach on native species. At the same time, some native plants that have disappeared from the area are being reintroduced.

Also, exotic mammals like Spanish goats and feral hogs become a nuisance. If allowed to run free, they tend to eliminate native species.

"Anybody who knows anything about the plants of Texas," Warren continued, "will be really interested in this area because there are more than 420 species in the park. That's pretty phe-

Vernal pools, depressions that collect soil and rainwater, are home to vegetation such as bellflower, wild onion, and lichens, as well as to the rare fairy shrimp.—Jack Lewis

nomenal for a sixteen-hundred-acre area. We have desert and wetland species because there is both shade and southern exposure. Water that's caught in the boulders and cracks supports species you won't find a mile from the park."

The park shelters several plants that grow in only a few places in Texas and are either rare or nonexistent elsewhere in the United States. For example, the basin bellflower, *Campanula reverchonii*, is abundant in the Central Mineral Region on slopes similar to the granite formations at Enchanted Rock. The only place it grows in the whole world is in the Central Mineral Region, and the only place it is protected is at Enchanted Rock.

Vernal pools, depressions in the granite of Enchanted Rock that im-

pound rain and soil, have permitted the tenuous evolution of more than one hundred forms of plant life. The pools represents miniature natural laboratories invaluable to scientific research. Entomologists, botanists, and ecologists all have an interest in the evolution of life taking place in these pools.

Later, while driving home, I thought about Grandma Rosa and Warren Watson. Grandma was from a world that passed away; Warren, firmly rooted in the present, held a vision for the future. Both shared a special reverence for Enchanted Rock and an abiding interest in native plants. And both of them understood the value of maintaining the natural balance. They were shaped by the land in much the same way the changing seasons formed Enchanted Rock.

Westcave

HOWARD PEACOCK

"What did the Indians hear?"

A class of sixth-graders sat cross-legged on the floor of the cave, becoming silent, listening intently. Some closed their eyes; others peered through the cave's opening to a lacy green world of trees and flowers, all hidden from the hot surface of the earth they knew.

John Ahrns softly repeated the question: "What did the Indians hear?"

Tall, lanky, tanned, Ahrns has spent years taking school children, ecologists, photographers, tourists, retirees, and other groups of one stripe or another down the trail and into the canyon of Westcave Preserve. He may spend more years or a whole lifetime doing the same; any person with a bent for nature would discover daily pleasures and challenges. None would doubt that Westcave Preserve is a surprising and compelling place.

Located about thirty-two miles or forty minutes west of Austin, next to a stretch of the Pedernales River, the Preserve contains thirty acres set aside in 1974 for posterity. Owned by the Lower Colorado River Authority, the Preserve is managed by a nonprofit, tax-exempt body, the Westcave Preserve Corporation.

Half the Preserve is Hill Country meadowland, mottled by live oak and juniper, or cedar as it's called, bejewelled with wildflowers in the springtime, abuzz with summer's insects. Rocks pile up here and there—skeltered limestone with cactus and seedlings growing in the crannies.

"At one time, this area was thick with grasses," Ahrns says. "Two hundred years ago, it made fine habitat for antelope, buffalo, and deer. Not so now." Years before the thirty acres

Water drips through an algae-encrusted rock.—Bill Reaves

became a preserve, it was severely over-grazed by cattle. So were the surrounding miles. Real estate developers are now circling the entire area.

The Westcave trail takes visitors through a meadow marked by agarita and Mexican persimmon to a deck overlooking a valley of the Pedernales River. The river rises from springs about 120 miles northward and joins the Colorado River 8 miles south of the Preserve. Back in 1952, the river flooded seventy feet above the old bridge here. The next day, Lake Travis rose forty-

Moist habitats of Westcave are favored by amphibians like the tiny cricket frog (Acris genus) who sits in gas bubbles from the algae.—Bill Reaves

five feet. Wild storms flay these hills and claim lives almost every year.

Just past the deck, the trail begins a long easy descent.

"Maybe fifty thousand years ago, certainly a long time ago, the canyon was formed when erosion cut sand and shale deposits from a limestone layer," Ahrns says. "The limestone collapsed and created a semitropical terrarium."

Both the plant community and the temperature change as a rude staircase with a railing leads visitors to the canyon floor. At the beginning of the descent, noticeable trees are live oak, shin oak, cedar elm, mesquite, Ashe juniper. Farther down, the trees become pecan, walnut, willow, box elder, sycamore, cypress, and at least eight other moisture-loving species. Shade deepens and the air cools. Ferns and mosses mass on the slopes.

"Wildlife has more protection as the growth becomes dense," Ahrns points out. "Food becomes accessible for more species. We've seen fox, coyote, bobcat, snakes, squirrel, owls—many species of birds, in fact." The Preserve is especially rich in golden-cheeked warblers.

Wild columbine forms colonies along the trail. Ahrns says that one species of *Salvia* thought to be extinct

was rediscovered a few years ago only forty feet from the trail.

A small creek flows along the lower path. Its source becomes evident at the head of the canyon.

Suddenly, as hikers round a curve, a huge, gnarled-root cypress stands in a vignette from a childhood fairy tale, rising in furrowed majesty past caves and limestone ledges to the open ground, now invisible one hundred feet above. At the base of the cypress, a small, white sand beach glistens in a shaft of sunlight beside a pool. Thin streams of spring water free-fall thirty feet into the pool from a fissure in the limestone.

There are places here to sit, rest, and look.

Behind the waterfall, a small cave beckons curious trail-walkers. From there, Ahrns leads the group into a larger adjoining cave where school groups get more answers to questions and let their imaginations work.

The trail walk with a guide takes less than two hours. Absolute care is taken to protect the environment and its plants and creatures. "They live here," Ahrns said. "We're just visitors—guests, if you like."

Ahrns designed and cut the trail

into the limestone several years ago. Visitors are urged not to step off the path even for a photograph. Pets are not allowed on the trail or in the preserve, nor is the removal of any specimen of plant or rock. *Preserve* is the key word.

A college-trained environmentalist, long on natural and scientific ecology, Ahrns guides groups of school children and other organizations on weekdays and takes informal small groups on weekends. Those tours are limited to thirty persons. Latecomers must wait for the next tour. There's no charge for the tour—perhaps one of the world's great bargains—but since the Preserve depends entirely on contributions to meet expenses, most visitors leave donations at the gate. "Our net cost per visitor, we've learned, comes to just over five dollars," Ahrns says.

The way to the gate is neither easy nor difficult. Leave Austin on South Lamar Street to the community of Oak Hill, then take State Highway 71 west through Bee Cave. Not far west you will see FM 3238 on the left. It is also the road to another delight of the Hill Country, Hamilton's Pool. About twelve miles from the turnoff, you cross the Pedernales River and come to Westcave Preserve.

History buffs also enjoy nearby Cypress Mill, founded and built by Mormons in the early 1840s to mill cypress wood for marketing in Marble Falls and Llano. At one time the town boomed, with a store, school, and bowling alley beside the mill.

Hammett's Crossing, right on the river, has a history, too. Washington

Walnuts, mulberries, elms, and a six-hundred-year-old cypress thrive in the environment of the preserve.—Bill Reaves

Hammett put in the crossing in the 1870s to save travelers a half-day on trips between Austin and Llano, and to make money for himself besides. In 1924, Travis County built a bridge at the crossing.

Those are places of this world, places of commerce and busy people. The cave in the collapsed grotto is of another time and dimension.

"What did the Indians hear?" Ahrns asks the young students a third time, the words barely audible. The children listen. For some, it may be the first time in their waking lives without the noise of a television or radio or people talking or traffic or a jukebox or factory whir or the general staccato hub-bub that presses upon life in the city and suburbs. "They heard birds," a boy says. "Happy birds." But he is the only one who speaks in the silence of the cave and the green canyon.

Indians heard the same birdsong, then others, and more. Something now rustles among leaves on the forest floor. A twig falls from the old cypress. Persistently, spring water spatters from the high ledge into the pool. . . .

Compelling sounds here. Serene sounds. For the Indians of past centuries. For today's near-deafened children. For all others who let go for a while and, wordless, simply listen.

Aransas: Showcase for Wildlife

Story and photographs by
RANDY GREEN

A few miles east of Texas Highway 35 between Aransas Pass and Port Lavaca, you can discover one of the most unusual wildlife sanctuaries in the United States, the Aransas National Wildlife Refuge. Most people associate the refuge with the whooping crane, and probably most visit for just one reason: to catch a glimpse of the magnificent bird that only a few years ago had scientists and conservationists wringing their hands over its fate.

Although the whooping cranes provided the initial reason for establishing a refuge on the peninsula, the choice proved a happy one for many other species as well. Another endangered bird, the Attwater's prairie chicken, also resides on the refuge's coastal prairie. Extensive hunting during the last century and habitat loss because of settlement and cultivation during this century almost wiped out this subspecies.

Visitors scanning the marshes for the more striking whoopers and the spectacular numbers of wintering waterfowl usually miss seeing the prairie chicken. Although one whole area of the refuge, the Tatten Addition, is devoted mainly to the chicken, glimpses are rare at Aransas, and visitors have better chances of seeing it on the Attwater Prairie Chicken Refuge near Eagle Lake.

Powerful fliers, whooping cranes make their first journey to Aransas from Alberta, Canada, when they are just a few months old.

The prairie chicken's scarcity is not mimicked by other species on the refuge. From November to April, thousands of ducks and geese cover the marshes. Waders like egrets, herons, spoonbills, and ibises line the shores of the bays and inland ponds. And wildlife is not confined to the marshes and bays. Aransas supports a staggering deer population despite constant efforts to trap and hunt the excess. A cool, clear winter day provides a good chance to see bucks sparring on the open grass savannas.

The savanna and live oak woodlands also support large numbers of wild turkey and javelina. Predators are less visible, but they are there, nonetheless. Coyote, bobcat, and recently

Snow geese wing their way to an evening's roost. →

Live oaks interspersed with grasslands grow on the higher portions of the refuge. The grass in the foreground is mostly bushy bluestem.

cougar and jaguarundi, a small dark cat usually found in the brush country of South Texas and Mexico, have been reported.

Visitors have easy access to some of the best areas on the refuge for viewing wildlife. A tour road skirts San Antonio Bay past inland pools and through the woodlands and savannas of the interior. An observation tower sits at one end of Mustang Lake. It offers visitors a good chance to see whooping cranes as well as other wading birds and waterfowl.

For those who want to experience Aransas through senses other than sight alone, a network of foot trails leads along marshes and ponds,

through live oak thickets, and among sand dunes long since overtaken by red bay and oak.

Since the whoopers frequently supplement their aquatic diet with acorns and other foods in the uplands but need open spaces to feed, refuge workers often burn large areas to keep oak thickets from taking over the grasslands. In this way they duplicate the action of natural fires that swept the region prior to settlement. In an experimental program, cattle are allowed to graze periodically in portions of the uplands, much as buffalo might have done before this century.

The prairie chickens benefit from similar treatment of their habitat, but

An old live oak overlooks San Antonio Bay.

here the objective is not to eliminate live oaks (of which there are few or none), but to discourage gulf cordgrass in favor of bluestems or forbs. Cordgrass is too dense for the prairie chickens and provides no food.

With the exception of an annual deer hunt to thin the whitetail population, the rest of the animals on the refuge are on their own. Alligator numbers have climbed, as has the population of brown pelicans. The pelicans' troubles were chiefly caused by poisoning from DDT, which has abated in recent years. The wide range of habitat — wetlands, woodlands, and savanna — lends importance to Aransas as a link in the chain of national wildlife refuges.

Habitat diversity makes possible species diversity, because different types of environment provide more places for more animals to live out their lives.

The worldwide plague of habitat destruction hasn't spared the Gulf Coast; every year more marshes are drained, coastlines developed, and prairies plowed. But refuges like Aransas remain a last line of defense of wildlife against rapidly expanding human population.

Padre Island

HOWARD PEACOCK

Waves and wind built Padre Island, a strip of sand 113 miles long between Port Isabel at the southern tip of Texas and the city of Corpus Christi. To the east rolls the Gulf of Mexico; westward, Laguna Madre shimmers in the brassy sun and mirrors the moon. Padre is the barrier between the Gulf and inland bays and rivers. On the strip, dunes vary from skinny to 3 miles wide. The whole process of island building began about three thousand years ago.

They say a treasure of eighty thousand dollars in cash plus an emerald necklace, all stuffed in a screwtop jar, lies beneath the sands somewhere on the island. It was buried by John Singer near a gale-blown tree when he took his family away from their ranch in 1861. When the family returned after the Civil War, the tree had vanished, all marks were covered up, and the dune-piled jar remains screwed tight. That's one treasure of Padre Island.

Today, treasures of a different kind reveal themselves constantly, if briefly. In season, the island sparkles with beach morning glories, Mexican primroses, firewheels, goldenrod, daisies, crotons, gentians, and sunflowers. Grains of sand heap together grasses

A lone piece of driftwood, once a tree on some distant southern shore, awaits discovery at Padre Island National Seashore.
—Jack Lewis

Branches of a lone stand of oaks point permanently in the direction of the prevailing winds.—Jack Lewis

Beach morning-glory covers the sand dunes of Padre Island with blooms from spring through fall. The flowers open each morning and close in the afternoon.—Jack Lewis

and sedges, sea oats, dollarworts, and cattails. Sea grape trails through the dunes. Only tough plants can survive the Gulf storms and blowing sands, the drenching rains that hit in huge drops, thirty-seven inches a year, and long weeks of drought.

Laughing gulls and egrets soar above the beaches and pick their way among the shallows. Falcons, hawks, owls, pelicans, roseate spoonbills, and scores of other bird species feed and breed in the teeming waters and wetlands.

Pompano, flounder, sheepshead, redfish, trout, drum, and mullet are among six hundred to eight hundred kinds of fishes that scientists say frequent the offshore waters. Tales describe tarpon and five-hundred-pound jewfish. Sev-

enty miles east, Sigsbee Deep stretches three hundred miles long and one hundred miles wide, big enough to enfold three Grand Canyons at a depth of twelve thousand feet.

Skeletons litter the beaches—the bones and abandoned homes of cockles and clams, scallops and sea horses, sand dollars and sea beans, whelks and coquinas, and prized snails like the olive and murex.

Seaward, Atlantic bottle-nosed dolphins frolic. Less often noted are pilot and pygmy whales, even an occasional blue whale.

Onshore, coyotes howl on most warm nights, and daylight picks out the tracks of raccoons and moles, jackrabbits, and perhaps bobcat and white-tailed deer.

All these evidences of nature on Padre Island testify to the power of recuperation. The island is recovering from years of relentless battering and a time of direct bombing.

Hurricanes come and go, and they can be expected to mess up and rearrange the face of the island. Making a comeback from human depredations is another matter. Cattle and horses overgrazed the island for decades. During World War II, the dunes served as targets for bombing practice by U.S. Navy air cadets. In recent times, hotels and condominiums have been built on the sands, and scores of thousands of merrymakers annually flock to the beaches, scattering and mounding their own spoor of summer.

Just in time, a bill creating the Padre Island National Seashore was passed in by the U.S. Congress, affording some protection for 130,697 acres of island nature.

"About 95 percent of the vegetation has returned," a ranger of the National Park Service recently estimated. "But it will take another two hundred years for the vegetation to grow back to what it should be."

Two hundred years. That's the prediction if nature's ways can run their course without serious human plundering and spoilage in the interim.

Singer's eighty thousand dollars in cash and necklace may easily be the least of Padre Island's hoard. Though its legends of shipwrecks and Karankawas and buried cash and jewels are valued pieces of Padre Island's past, its real treasure comes to life every day among the sands, sedges, and flowers, in the sky and dark blue waters.

Gulls at Padre spend all their time eating or looking for food.—Jack Lewis

Grassy vegetation along Mustang Island slows erosion and acts as a windbreak that gently catches the blowing sand.—Jack Lewis →

PART II

Every Living Thing

In whose hand is the soul of every living thing. . . .
                                        —JOB 12:10

Exotic creatures injected Texas talk with graphic lyricism and originality of expression. Encountering a bizarre, knobby reptile skittering across their homesteads, settlers called the creature a Texas horned toad, frog, or lizard.—Glen Mills, Texas Parks & Wildlife Department

Classic Critters

HOWARD PEACOCK

The Texas Horned Toad

No matter how much you admire pure ugliness, do not take a horned toad home. In Texas, which appreciates the grotesque along with the glorious, this beast is protected by law.

The Texas horned toad (*Phrynosoma cornutum*) is not a toad at all, but a lizard. It looks a lot like a cactus. It runs remarkably fast on short legs and squirts blood from its eyes.

This reptilian legend can be found in open terrain of sand, rock, even loamy soil at altitudes ranging from sea level to six thousand feet or higher. It requires warmth, ants, and crannies in which to hide from hawks, roadrunners, whipsnakes, and collard lizards, all of which eat the Texas horned toad. While ants constitute its favorite meal, the Texas horned toad will also eat spiders, sowbugs, and other insects. It drinks morning dew on plant leaves in the desert and elsewhere to slake its thirst.

Monster movies often show the Texas horned toad close up, its grisly profile exaggerated to giant proportions, those two spiked horns aimed at demolishing cities and civilizations. Actually, it is only about four inches long. The world record is, or was, seven and one-eighths inches.

Who would want to carry such a beast home? Many tourists would—many unknowing tourists and unmannerly children. But the Texas horned toad craves freedom so ardently that it usually dies in any kind of captivity.

The female, beautiful in the eyes of the beholding male, in the springtime lays two dozen eggs—yellowish orbs with tough leathery shells. They hatch promptly. When winter comes, the animal crawls underground into a burrow and sleeps until spring. Then it moves out into the warm sun and sheds its old skin. In its new finery, which may be reddish, brownish, grayish, or muddy mustard, it begins the courting process and the cycle repeats itself.

This lizard's trick of spewing blood comes from a peculiar ability to increase blood pressure in its head. When threatened or aggravated, the Texas horned toad flicks its tail like a mad cat, puffs itself out, lowers its head to present horns like bayonets, and from the corners of its eyes shoots a fine spray of crimson. The spray may travel for several feet and scare the bejabbers out of the tormentor.

Señor Coyote

Is the coyote the most intelligent animal of the Texas wild? The wiliest? The biggest pest? An efficient and benevolent control on rodents and other varmints? The most freedom-loving creature of all?

Superlatives about the coyote seem to go to the limits of the language—or rather the languages, Indian, Spanish, and English alike. Many cultures have alternately praised and despised *Canis latrans*, the "prairie wolf."

Even the range of this breed starts arguments. If you told a friend today what you know its range to be, you would be wrong by noon tomorrow. In Texas, coyotes trot around just about every county. In the other states they howl at concerts in the Hollywood Bowl and at the lapping of waves on old Maine's shores. You will find coyotes from Alaska to Guatemala. Some maps don't show them in Southeastern states yet, but mind the "yet." Coyotes can travel when the notion strikes. They are known at altitudes extending from sea level to mountains over ten thousand feet high.

The coyote cry is perhaps the most characteristic cry of the Western Plains. It yaps, yips, weeps, laughs, and howls in response to human song and invention, from Tannhauser to train whistles.

Coyote lore harks back to the Aztecs, who worshiped a god named Coyotlinauatl and who gave the animal its root name, *coyotl*. Modern Mexicans use "coyote" to identify a sly crook, or, in another sense, to marvel at a person's general intelligence—"*muy coyote*," they might say.

"The coyote can stare a bird right out of a tree," one belief attests. If the prairie wolf can't get the bird's attention by hypnotic eye-contact, it will grab its tail and spin 'round and 'round, causing the prey in the tree to get so dizzy that it topples to the ground.

Freedom seems more important to the coyote than to many other creatures. Mindless of pain, it will chew off its own legs or paws to escape from a trap. "I'll never put out another trap," a Texas farmer told writer Barbara Wesolek. He had found a chewed-off paw in the steel. "Anything that set on being free shouldn't be destroyed by me. It's like killing what I myself hold most dear."

Weighing about thirty pounds, fat at thirty-five, smaller than a red wolf, the coyote stretches out to about three feet in length. Its usual color is buffy above and whitish below, with a black tip on the tail. The legs are earth-colored, but colors and patterns vary. Coyotes breed with other canines, and a lot of shades and tones get scrambled.

Coyotes don't care much what kind of food grows or runs about the terrain. They eat snakes, frogs, fruits, vegetables, rabbits, rodents, birds, skunks, weasels, shrews, moles, garbage, goats, poultry, old or crippled livestock, lizards, carrion—whatever comes to view when one is hungry.

Controversy surrounds the coyote. Ranchers and farmers complain that the animal preys on their livestock and poultry. But one scientist identified the contents of 8,339 coyote stomachs from the American West and found that more than three-fourths of the contents were composed of rabbits, rodents, and carrion.

A strong family sense keeps coyotes from being gregarious, although several families might hunt big game together, then disband when the hunt is over. Many observers believe the male and female of a family will pair for life.

Alone in the deepening dusk, a coyote begins to yowl its eerie song.—Wyman Meinzer

The Texas hare was called a jackass rabbit because of its jackass-like ears. Ranchers have clocked jackrabbits running alongside their pickups at forty miles per hour.
—Bill Reaves

If you are not convinced that coyotes are smart, observe the relay race a family organizes to catch a speedier jackrabbit. Jackrabbits race at over forty miles an hour, leaving a hungry coyote pooped at thirty-five. However, when the original chaser tires, it will drive the rabbit toward a stand of brush, from which explodes a fresh coyote to continue the chase. The pooped coyote follows at a leisurely pace, regaining breath and stamina, then hides in cross-lot brush or a clump of high grass ready to spring anew at the prey whizzing by. The jackrabbit is soon exhausted by such maneuvers.

Once the quarry of wolves, which have been exterminated in most of Texas and the vast rangelands, coyotes now fear only humankind as their enemies and predators.

Jack

The jackrabbit got its popular name from a pioneer inclination to call anything with long ears a "jackass." Soon the appellation was shortened to "jack rabbit." The creature we know as such is not a real rabbit, that term being properly reserved for small European burrowing animals that produce naked young. All the rabbits in North America are hares. They do not burrow, and their young are born hairy.

Jackrabbits (*Lepus californicus*) range through the western two-thirds of Texas and far past those borders, too. They don't favor coniferous forests except for the relatively small stands of piñon pines and junipers of the west. They want open country where their extraordinarily long hind legs can blow past many a predator and where their exceptional hearing and eyesight can work at maximum power.

Jacks are not only famous for their speed, up to forty-five miles per hour, but also for their getaway. *Ka-pow!* That fast, it leaps in high bounds from a hiding place. However, if its stringy chops are being coveted by a hungry coyote, Jack forgoes the dramatics and races away with ears flattened.

Despite its charm and heroics in cartoons, the jackrabbit poses a serious problem to ranchers. Fields already overgrazed by livestock are depleted further by jack's preference for areas of sparse vegetation.

Jack spends much of each day dozing under scrub or in a clump of grass that offers some protection from summer's sun and winter's winds. At twilight, jack begins foraging and carrying on. Besides forage crops, jackrabbits eat cactus, sagebrush, grasses, herbs, and mesquite beans.

The world-famous breeding season for jack extends from December to September in Texas. About a month and a half after breeding takes place, a litter of one to a half-dozen young are born. Two to six litters may be produced each year. Such figures cause computers to throw springs and jam the gears.

Riddle of the Ridley

"Capable of almost manic violence when captured," says the authoritative *Running Press Book of Turtles*, speaking of the Atlantic Ridley turtle, one of the most endangered species on earth and a citizen of the Gulf waters off Texas.

"It can devote remarkable strength to attacking those who attempt to lay hold of it," the book continues. "Reportedly, they never seem to lose their wariness and always sleep with their eyes open."

Humans have been laying hold of the Atlantic Ridley's destiny in gross ignorance or greed since 1950. That was the year when, after centuries of mystery and scientific puzzlement, the only breeding place of this rare creature was discovered on a section of uninhabited beach in Mexico. A few individuals, it was later found, may also nest near Padre Island on the Texas coast.

The location was "immediately, disastrously pillaged," writes author R. E. Nicholls. Nesting females were slaughtered for their eggs, not just once but for years afterward. Poachers began capturing the egg-heavy females even while the animals in the sea struggled toward shore to lay their eggs. They then broke the turtles apart to scoop out the eggs to sell for soup.

Once there were forty thousand females at an *arribada*, or nesting. By 1967, only some twenty-two hundred turtles were counted.

Why save the Atlantic Ridley? Well, why save the whooping crane, or the ivory-billed woodpecker, or any other creature or plant on the globe? Many people argue, isn't it only an animal or a plant?

Experts on the Atlantic Ridley and other rare species point out that plants and animals are also occupants of this life-sphere. They occupy their own particular niche in the grand scheme of life. This is their home, too. Does superior brain power give humans the right to destroy other life-forms indiscriminately, if at all?

Indeed, plants and animals tell scientists when air, water, and soil are poisoned by pollution or nonbiodegradable plastics or just stupid negligence. Most of humankind's medicines developed from plants and animals, and still develop from them today. Even petroleum molecules, the basic stuff of modern healing pharmaceuticals, once were living tissues.

Ranging from the Gulf of Mexico up the coastline shallows of the eastern United States, the Atlantic Ridley (*Lepidochelys kempii*) is the smallest of the sea turtles and is also known as the "bastard turtle," a name stemming from a mistaken idea that the species is a cross between the green turtle and the loggerhead. Parts of its coastal habitat have been spoiled by overfishing and beach garbage.

The Atlantic Ridley can be recognized by its gray carapace, which may be either heart-shaped or round, and five large side-plates on each side. Two similar species, the green and hawksbill, have only four. A Pacific Ocean turtle, *Lepidochelys olivacea*, is similar in virtually all respects except color, it being distinctively olive. The Atlantic Ridley measures up to 29½ inches long. It weighs about one hundred pounds at maturity. Mollusks, crustaceans, jellyfish, and sea urchins make up its

diet, but crabs are its favorite meals.

Can the Atlantic Ridley, a bell-wether of the ocean environment in Texas and elsewhere, survive the human onslaught? When its only nesting beach in existence was discovered, Mexico stationed troops with submachine guns to protect the area. Laws still warn the ignorant and the greedy. But poachers still laugh at the laws. Little wonder, then, that the Ridley instinctively grows "manic" in its violence when taken into captivity.

The Ridley turtle is a seriously endangered species.—Bill Reaves, Texas Parks & Wildlife *Magazine*

Old-timers gave the roadrunner its name because of the way it darted across the brushland and dusty by-ways.—Jack Lewis

King of the Road

BOB GATES

Beep-Beep! Zooom_____!

A blur flashes across the screen, vainly pursued by a not-too-bright coyote. The confused coyote will never prevail, for it is chasing the fabled roadrunner.

This is the way life is for the star of the Warner Brothers cartoon series, "The Roadrunner." But what of the *real* roadrunner, that rangy character that lives among the mesquite and prickly pear of the Southwest?

He is a member of the cuckoo family. He can run ten to twenty miles an hour; averages twenty-two inches in length (half of that is tail); feeds on snakes, lizards, and large insects; and produces two broods a year from four to nine eggs.

Maybe the reason the coyote has such a rough time is because it is difficult to tell from the roadrunner's tracks which way he is going. Two of his toes point forward and two point backward, a characteristic peculiar to members of the cuckoo family.

Contrary to cartoon lore, the roadrunner can fly adequately. He must want to give his pursuers a sporting chance, though, because he usually makes his getaway on those crazy cuckoo feet. He does his running in Texas, New Mexico, Arizona, California, and most of Mexico and into Colorado, Oklahoma, and Kansas.

The name "roadrunner," according to the *Encyclopaedia Britannica*, was awarded to the crafty critter during the horse-and-buggy days because he liked to race carriages. Depending on the locale, his other monikers are *paisano* (fellow-countryman) and chaparral. In the scientific community, he is *Geococcyx californianus*.

At one time, people thought the roadrunner ate young birds, since he was known to chase quail chicks. Closer observation has proved that the chase was to feed on the grasshoppers and other insects stirred up by the running chicks. In her book *Desert Mavericks*, Eve Garson describes his real fare:

. . . in his gizzard—if you please—
Are lizards, rats, and bumble bees;
Also horned toads—on them he feeds—
And rattlesnakes! and centipedes!

Notice that last line—rattlesnakes and centipedes. The fact that the roadrunner kills rattlesnakes has probably done more for his image in folklore as a bird of good fortune than any other single thing.

Tales of the endearing qualities of the roadrunner place him third as a favorite in frontier and Indian folklore, following only the eagle and the turkey. The Tarahumara Indians of Mexico, the great cross-country runners, hold the belief that the meat of the roadrunner passes on to them the bird's great strength in running. Early ranchers believed that one of the best cures for "Job's curse" (boils) was a hearty meal of boiled *paisano*. His feathers decorated the legs of Indian runners as an assurance of speed and endurance. The fringe that adorns the leggings of some Indians is said to be a copy of the feathers of the roadrunner, intended to ward off snakes.

New Mexico's Pueblo Indians believed that the track of the roadrunner, mimicked on the ground around the tent of a dead person, would mislead evil spirits. The mothers of the tribe also tied the bird's feathers to their babies' cradleboards to confuse evil spirits. In parts of Mexico, the roadrunner, not the stork, brings babies into the world. The Plains Indians used the whole skin of what they called the medicine bird as a totem over the lodge door to fend off unfavorable gods.

In various parts of Mexico, the *paisano* is viewed as a trailblazer for anyone lost in the wilderness. Following a roadrunner will lead a lost person to a trail. Why? The roadrunner prefers trails and follows them to feed on the tumblebugs that are to be found in the droppings of pack animals.

An old Spanish legend that tells a story of misfortune explains how the roadrunner got both its name and its character. Early Spanish settlers referred to the roadrunner as *faisan reál* (royal pheasant). The name reflected the behavior of the bird as he strutted about the countryside obviously pleased with himself. This vanity developed to such a point that he would not speak to such common birds as the sparrow, wren, and dove. The more brightly colored birds he addressed as *paisano*.

One day as the King of Birds was discussing the problem of the roadrunner's vanity, the roadrunner ambled into the proceedings unannounced and with extreme familiarity addressed the group, "How fare my countrymen? And my *paisanos* all, how are you?" This pompous conduct infuriated the king, and he ordered, "Out of my presence, you low-born thing of the ground! Never again presume to be a *faisan*. Henceforth, stay on the ground where you belong. Forget to fly. Feed on tarantulas, scorpions, and beetles." The roadrunner tried to fly from the room, but his wings had lost their strength. Since that time, the roadrunner has been called *paisano* as a reminder of his presumption.

Not all stories about the roadrunner originate in the wickiup or tepee. Tales of the roadrunner's fight for survival are also related by those who share his range as they work the ranches of West and South Texas. In an article entitled "The Roadrunner in Fact and Folk-Lore," J. Frank Dobie relates many stories as fact and presents others that must be told with a bit of a smile. One of his stories is about a roadrunner that kept a hill of lizards, something like a lizard-tail farm. The idea was simple enough. The roadrunner supposedly discovered that if he snapped off the tail of a lizard, the lizard promptly grew another that was just as tasty as the original.

Numerous stories tell of the roadrunner's snake-snaring "corral of thorns," a wall of cholla cactus that the roadrunner builds around a sleeping rattlesnake. The rattler is then rudely awakened when the roadrunner drops a

Roadrunner parents take turns hunting for food for their young. Here, one of the adults feeds a Texas horned lizard to the nestlings.—Wyman Meinzer, Texas Parks & Wildlife *Magazine*

cholla joint on his head. Agitated by the harassing roadrunner, the striking rattler soon impales himself on the biting cholla thorns and can offer little defense to the piercing thrust of the roadrunner's lethal beak.

Another story has it that the roadrunner will fight the rattler by dangling a prickly pear pad in his beak as a shield against the striking snake. After a few head-long jabs at this thorned thwarter, the enraged rattler gives up, no match for the cunning roadrunner.

Texas tall tales? They could be, but it is true that the roadrunner fights the serpent, without the aid of thorn or shield. His combat is conducted in true matador manner. With wings outstretched, feathers flexing, eye-to-eye contact, he moves at the instant of the snake's strike, to offer the rattler's

fangs only empty feathers and dust. The empty cape of the roadrunner, like that of the matador, drives his opponent to exhaustion. The thrust of the swordlike bill should be driven home to the cheers of *Olé!* In the arena of the dense chaparral he is El Matador Magnifico.

Today the roadrunner is still an active part of the arid Texas landscape, a not-so-simple cuckoo that now and then chases a horseless carriage, fights a few rattlesnakes, eats a lizard or two, and in animated antics darts through the chaparral, calling "crut-crut-crut." The country and the climate are harsh, but left to his element the roadrunner holds his own in the scheme of things.

Little else need be said to those who know him, for to them he is truly *paisano*—fellow countryman.

Where Birds Fly

JACK LOWRY

Sheer size makes Texas a birder's paradise, but perhaps just as important is the state's location at the meeting ground of East and West, North and South, highlands and lowlands, humidity and aridity.

Each spring, birders from all over the country flock to the Texas coast to witness the massive migrations of scarlet tanagers, indigo buntings, gray catbirds, grosbeaks, orioles, warblers, and vireos as they reach the first landfall after their long flight across the Gulf of Mexico.

Birding authority Victor Emanuel of Austin takes groups every April to High Island, northeast of Galveston. From there, day trips include part of the Big Thicket National Preserve to see such rarities as the red-cockaded woodpecker; the Anahuac National Wildlife Refuge, where rails, coots, terns, and herons can be found; and the Bolivar Peninsula, which has one of the greatest concentrations of shorebirds in North America.

"We stay in one place, which is possible only in a few rich areas of the country, like the Texas coast," Emanuel says. "We plan the tour to intersect with the Gulf Coast migration."

The best time to see migrating birds in the High Island area is mid-April to mid-May. Birders at High Island hope for bad weather. After a rainshower, or with the arrival of a cold front, the phenomenon called "fallout" occurs. Following their long flight across the Gulf,

thousands of exhausted birds literally fall out of the sky and dive for the cover of the thick hackberry, sycamore, water oak, and live oak groves at High Island, which stands above the surrounding coastal belt. If the weather is good, the birds find shelter and food in a number of wooded areas, so the spectacle is less impressive.

Fields along the coast also attract a variety of migrating birds. At the end of April and in early May, the rare Hudsonian godwit feeds in Texas rice fields after its flight from South America. On one drive between Houston and High Island, Emanuel and his colleague John Rowlett spotted 350 Hudsonian godwits in one rice field. Since then, they have heard reports of more than a thousand in a field. "Only in Texas can you see these concentrations," he says. Once the godwits replenish themselves and regain their energy, they disperse and head for their breeding grounds in northwestern Canada.

Laughing gulls are common along the Texas Gulf coast. The adults are easily identified by the black hood and dark gray back and wings.—Bill Reaves

The scarlet tanager winters in Texas. —John Tveten

83

The American egret has made a dramatic comeback after its numbers were drastically reduced by plume hunters at the turn of the century.—Randy Green

Scissor-tailed flycatchers can be seen along most roads. Their diet includes many insects that are harmful to agriculture.—Bill Reaves

Like the birds they watch, birders return to High Island year after year. "It's one of the most exciting migration situations anywhere," says Emanuel. "It's as good as any area in the world." All-time bird authority Roger Tory Peterson agrees. He says the spring fallout in Texas must be seen to be believed.

Along the Texas coast, birders never know what special treats to expect. On a recent April tour, birders came upon a flock of gulls bathing at a pond near High Island. They saw the five common Texas gulls—laughing, herring, ring-billed, Bonaparte's, and Franklin's. "Then we spotted a black-legged kitti-wake and Thayer's gull, both of which are rare in this area," Emanuel says.

"Later, as we were driving toward the Bolivar Peninsula, John stopped his van to talk to some friends from California who hoped to see the two rare gulls at the pond, but had no luck.

"I was behind them and saw a very large gull flying over John's van. I got on the CB to John and said, 'There's a lesser black-backed gull over your van!' Suddenly, an explosion of excited people piled out of the van. Our friends from California didn't know what was going on."

"Birds are everywhere, so a birder always has something to do," Emanuel observes. "A birder would never be bored. Birds attract us because they're visible. Their migrations fascinate us. We're part of the same world."

Good tours put people in touch with more than just birds. They provide a complete nature experience, including habitats, other animals, wildflowers, and the interactions between humans and the natural world.

Winged Beauties

Story and photographs by
GEYATA AJILVSGI

While botanizing in Texas in 1828, the Swiss naturalist Jean Louis Berlandier wrote of his April trek from Bexar to Gonzales as among "rolling hills, woods, and small valleys bedecked with beautiful flowers, where numerous butterflies flitted about making the solitary region all the more charming."

Berlandier's mention of the butterflies he encountered comes as no surprise to today's roamer of the roads, for wherever you go in Texas, these colorful winged beauties are almost constant companions.

With its varied habitats and climate, Texas offers unexcelled opportunities for the butterfly watcher. Many species reach their range limits within the confines of the state. Species from Florida and other southeastern states extend their range westward into the wooded eastern portion of our state and along the beaches and brackish marshes of the coastline. Other brilliantly hued species overflow from Mexico and the tropics into the Rio Grande Valley, Texas' richest area for rare and unusual butterflies.

Of the estimated fifteen thousand species of butterflies in the world, some seven hundred are native to North America. Texas ranks highest in the United States with more than four hundred species and subspecies, including nonresident strays from across the borders.

One of the most beautiful of Texas' four hundred species of butterflies, the question mark has deeply angled wings outlined in iridescent violet.

To keep tabs on the population and species present in local areas, the Xerxes Society, a nationwide group interested in endangered species and in butterflies particularly, initiated a butterfly count that is held annually throughout North America.

If you are a newcomer to the butterfly watching game, you need to remember that butterflies, like flowers, have their seasons. From the first warm days

The giant swallowtail is an easy-going but-terfly.

of spring until the first hard freeze of winter, different species appear at regular intervals. Some species will live for only a few days or weeks. Others can be seen flying throughout the warmer months, although they may be more plentiful at certain times. In the subtropical Rio Grande Valley, butterflies can be seen on the wing even during the winter, and the best time to find some of the less common ones is from October through December.

Especially good years for butterflies occur occasionally when environmental conditions are optimal. Moisture is needed to produce lush growth of larval food plants, yet the rainy season should not be so prolonged that the larvae are killed by viruses. Also, butterflies are more plentiful when a bumper crop of flowers has been produced. Areas where butterflies tend to congregate by the score are known as "hot spots." According to Dr. Raymond

Neck of the Texas Parks and Wildlife Department, these hot spots occur in disturbed areas where many weedy species bear nectar-producing flowers. As locations change ecologically, butterflies may not be found where they have been before.

The dazzling beauty of butterflies comes from the intricate patterns and colorations formed by the hairs that cover their bodies. The abdomen of a butterfly is almost always covered with soft, silky hairs, while the wings are covered with minute hairs modified into flat, overlapping scales.

Scales that cover the wings are usually the most showy, getting their coloring from pigmentation, ultramicroscopic refractional structures, or a combination of the two that creates a mosaic of flashing hues. Pigmental colors are the most common. They occur either from chemicals produced in the body of the insect or from the food plants of the larva. These chemicals within the scales absorb certain wavelengths of light and transmit others, which we see as colors.

Structural colors are more complex. They derive from scales with various striations that act as prisms, refracting sunlight and producing a spectacularly iridescent effect. Both kinds of scales that cover butterfly wings are easily rubbed off. When the insect is handled, scales look like fine dust or powder on the fingers.

Special scent scales also occur on the wings of male butterflies. Sometimes these scales are scattered randomly about the wing, but more often they

The painted lady ranges far and wide in its feeding.

cluster into showy eyespots or dots. Other times, the scent-producing apparatus is formed by long hairs gathered into small brushlike tufts. The tufts exude a most delightful perfume during courtship. These special scents of the males are often referred to as aphrodisiacs, but perhaps wrongly so, since the female may become either passive or excited before mating.

While flowers provide the common food of most butterflies, some species exhibit rather bizarre food preferences. They may seek out the sap of certain trees, fermented juices of rotting fruit or sugar cane, muddy water, or the noxious-smelling elixirs of garbage dumps and cattle pens.

Most butterflies will be found in open, sunny areas, but others can only be located among the leaf litter of the forest floor, among tall marsh grasses, or in the deep shade of junglelike palm and palmetto. Fortunately for interested travelers, butterflies often haunt roadsides because of the abundance of wildflowers there. National wildlife refuges are also excellent sites for butterfly watching.

Wherever we sight these fragile creatures, their delightful presence adds a special beauty to our day.

The buckeye has many regional and seasonal forms. A wary flyer, it can be seen near flowers or while poised for a drink in moist areas.

Orchids of the Big Thicket

HOWARD PEACOCK
AND ANNE GARNER

If you look at Joe Liggio's photographs on these pages and think to yourself, or even burst out loud and say, "Son of a gun, wish I could shoot pictures like that!"—take heart.

A while back, Joe wasn't sure which side of the camera to look through. Then some friends persuaded him to go on a field trip in the Big Thicket. He had heard about the Big Thicket since he was a boy in Galveston. He had read tales about the place in newspapers and magazines. But he didn't reckon on what he saw.

A hero of Big Thicketeers named Claude McLeod, a professor at Sam Houston State University in Huntsville, led the field trip that Joe and his friends joined. One of the places they went was a bog in Tyler County. It used to be known as Armand's Bog, after naturalist Armand Yramategui, who borrowed money to buy it before it was bulldozed and "developed."

In the bog that day, Joe saw his first *Calopogon* orchid, and it was virtually a turning point for him. The experience wasn't like Saul of Tarsus's being hit by a flash of light on the road to Damascus, but it wasn't more than two cuts down. Thousands of Big Thicket converts know the feeling. Joe bought a camera and started heading over to the Thicket on weekends.

A wild orchid is not just another pretty flower. You often have to suffer before you see them. Muddy feet and chiggers may be part of the price. If you don't like beech trees and blowing clouds, dark creeks and butt-sprung khakis, birds and bugs and nameless creatures, you'll never take memorable pictures in the Big Thicket.

Learn to look. Glance at the roadsides and into fields while you're driving. In the deep woods, peer past the leaves sponging the forest floor and beyond the trunks of the next neighborhood of trees.

Recently, poking around Jack Gore Baygall, Joe was marveling at the huge beeches, magnolias, and loblolly pines dominating the woods and bordering sloughs of the Neches River there in eastern Tyler County.

"I happened to look down and saw stalks of dried orchids on the forest floor," he says. "The seed pods told me that the stalks had been orchids. Fresh shoots came up at the bottom of the stalks. They looked like shoots of coral root orchids I'd seen on a vacation in the Rocky Mountains. The only orchid it could be was the crested coral root." He made notes, and the following year at blooming season for the species he went back to the exact spot to photograph the flower.

It is easy to get confused by common names of flowers. An orchid by a simi-

An orange plume orchid (Habenaria chapmanii) *bursts into bloom in Tyler County. Flowering July through August, the orange plume closely resembles the yellow fringed orchid* (Habenaria ciliaris).
—Joe Liggio

Also called the "cockscomb orchid," the crested coral root (Hexalectris spicata) grows up to 30 inches tall and blooms in moist pinelands during the summer months.—Joe Liggio

lar name, spring coral root, but not even in the same genus as the crested coral root, was once found in abundance at the Big Creek Scenic Area that is popular with Houston families. When the authorities began trying to eradicate the pine bark beetle, the orchids seemed to disappear. The connection is unclear, but for the past few years no spring coral root orchids have been found at the spot.

Speaking of names, why do they call *Pogonia ophioglossoides* the snakemouth orchid? Or adder's tongue, or adder's breath? Who ever got close enough on purpose to sniff a snake's breath? Be that as it may, snakemouths tend to come out in clumps after a burn. A burn is a prescribed fire set and controlled by experts in an ecosystem that has been almost overpowered by invading species of shrubs and small trees. Huge clumps of snakemouths have appeared in a pitcher plant bog after a burn in the Turkey Creek Unit of the Big Thicket National Preserve.

Sometimes looking and hoping and learning by studying books and doing fieldwork, all put together, do not amount to much. The Big Thicket is fickle, or seems so at times. The only thing a wild orchid seeker can do is to find a knowing friend.

"I'd been looking for the orange plume orchid for a couple of years," Joe says. "Just hadn't had any luck, even though I was poking around the right kinds of places." When he had exhausted all the possibilities he knew, he talked to Geraldine Watson, who ranks among the all-time great naturalists of the Big Thicket. She told him to go to a certain remote spot in Tyler County where he could likely find the orange plume orchid and the Carolina lily as well. That's where he took the picture of the orange plume shown here.

The most sought-after orchid in the Big Thicket is the yellow lady-slipper, a spectacular bloom that once was easily found in Newton County but now has been robbed of virtually all of its habitats in these parts. Osa Hall, a highly knowledgeable native of the upper eastern region of the Thicket, led Liggio to the picture you see here.

"Osa had heard about a proposed clear-cut in Newton County. He went out there and found a single yellow lady-slipper in the zone to be clear-cut," Joe relates. "Osa hadn't seen a specimen of this orchid growing wild in years. He dug it up before the bulldozers got to the spot. As soon as he got home, he planted it by a creek. It lived. Today, a clump of a couple dozen yellow lady-slippers thrives right there by his creek."

The wild orchid most often photographed in the Big Thicket is the *Calopogon*, or grass pink. Its beauty belies its common name. Droves of nature lovers come to the Thicket each springtime to see the *Calopogon*. Usually they go to spots where they saw it the preceding year. Too often, it is no longer there. Its habitats are being drained. Seeps, a favorite environment of the *Calopogon*, are being plowed up and paved. Two species of *Calopogon* live in the Thicket. The bearded grass pink,

Technically known as Calopogon pulchellus, *which means "little beauty," the grass pink rarely shows such an astonishing array of flowers. It prefers acid meadows and pinelands and blooms in the spring.—Joe Liggio*

Calopogon barbatus, is the smaller of the two, flowers earlier, and is classified as rare. As many as fifty have been found in the Kirby State Forest, but that was after a burn, when they are more numerous. No such luck has been reported since then.

The other grass pink species, *Calopogon pulchellus*, was a favorite of Henry David Thoreau, who wrote of it in his journals. The picture of it here was shot in 1980 on a damp slope near a privately owned lake. The stalk is highly unusual. Ordinarily, you find one or two flowers on a *Calopogon* stalk, and if two, one of them is declining. But this stalk has four flowers at the peak of their bloom at the same time. It's one of many surprises of extravagant beauty to be found in the wild.

The rare yellow lady-slipper (Cypripedium calceolus), *so-called because the petals cup to form a moccasin shape, is the largest of East Texas orchids. The slipper is about two and one-half inches long.*
—Joe Liggio

Barbed Beauty

FRANK BEESLEY

When Conard Jenkins climbed out of the prickly pear cactus where his horse had deposited him, he wasted no time getting out of his jeans and beginning the painful process of drawing stickers from his various parts.

He had been helping a friend and the friend's father brand calves. Seeing Conard's predicament, the father, a hard-boiled old rancher, drawled, "Here's the way to fix them cactus stickers, boy." He picked up a mesquite branch and rubbed Conard's legs and buttocks briskly, breaking off the hair-fine stickers at the skin's surface. "Now they won't catch on your clothes and aggravate you. The ends'll fester and back out right soon."

Conard would be hard to convince that prickly pears have any redeeming qualities, but the fact is, where it grows abundantly the prickly pear serves several important functions. Many wild creatures depend on this cactus for food, moisture, and cover.

Chuck Dalchau, a biologist for the Texas Parks and Wildlife Department, says that in South Texas prickly pear provide white-tailed deer with about 30 percent of their annual diet. But the Prickly Pear Pig title goes to the javelina (collared peccary). Its menu consists of more than 60 percent prickly pear cactus. Where these water-storing plants are plentiful, they may provide 100 percent of the javelina's water requirements.

Prickly pear cacti (Opuntia *sp.) adapt to their environment and cover huge ranges of territory.— Richard Reynolds,* Texas Dept. of Commerce

Other cactus users include wild turkeys, which eat the seeds; quail and other birds and small animals that use the sprawling thickets for cover; and even honey bees, which gather nectar and pollen from the large, showy blossoms. Cactus honey is full-flavored and turns ordinary bread into cake.

Texas cattle also have a fondness for prickly provender. Tommy Welch, extension range specialist at Texas A&M University, says that cattle often indicate a preference for cactus. "In times of drought when range grasses are scarce, ranchers commonly burn the thorns off the prickly pear on their range so the cattle can eat it. They use butane- or kerosene-fueled burners that work like flamethrowers to burn away the spines."

Prickly pear cacti have two types of stickers: regular spines about ¾ to 2½ inches long, and glochids (pronounced GLOW-kids). Glochids are nefarious little stickers this genus of cactus produces especially to bedevil unsuspecting human beings. They are from ⅛ to ⅝ of an inch long and individually nearly invisible, but when embedded in the sensitive flesh on the inside of the fingers they feel like fence posts.

Glochids grow in clusters around small oval openings (areoles) in the skin of the plant. They are loosely attached, and the slightest touch brings away a cluster that looks like a tuft of fine, brown hair.

Unlike most regular spines, glochids are barbed. Their barbs and their tiny size combine to make them difficult to extract from the skin. They tend to break off, leaving stubs that extend just enough above the surface to be a constant aggravation. The best way to cope with them is to shave the ends off with a sharp razor.

Prickly pear pads and fruit have been table fare for man in the Americas since before there were tables. The prickly pear fruit—called tunas—were especially popular with the Indians of Texas and Mexico before the Spanish arrived.

The Coahuiltecan Indians, a tribe that inhabited the Texas coast and all

In Texas, prickly pear cactus grows from the Gulf Coast near Aransas Bay to the far west. A distinctive member of the genus, Opuntia compressa, *grows in the Big Thicket of southeast Texas.—Jack Lewis*

of South Texas until they were devastated by Spanish-introduced diseases, preserved cactus tunas by squeezing out the juice and sun-drying them. Even the skins were saved, dried, and pounded into flour.

Spanish explorer Cabeza de Vaca said that the dried fruit was placed in "hampers like figs." Because of this widespread use of cactus tunas by the Indians, the fruits became known as Indian figs.

Gathering cactus tunas must have been a tough assignment for the Indian girls. They had no butane burners to use on the stickers. Apache legend has it that all cacti with edible fruit were covered with sharp spines that made it nearly impossible to pick the fruit. One of the Apache demigods, called Killer of Enemies, took pity on the people and by magic caused most of the stickers to disappear. One wonders why he didn't finish the job.

Despite the spines and glochids, modern folks follow the Indians' example and harvest prickly pears for a variety of uses. Sometimes in the spring, the new pads—called *nopalitos*, from *nopal*, the Spanish name for prickly pear—are picked before their tissues harden and before the spines and glochids are produced. These *nopalitos* can be breaded with cornmeal and fried, or they can be boiled, cut into chunks, and included in omelets.

Cactus country, according to a survey made by the Texas Agricultural Experiment Station in 1980, includes most of Texas. About 25.5 million acres of rangeland across the state have some prickly pear. Even the woods of the Big Thicket contain one species, *Opuntia compressa*. The Edwards Plateau and South Texas have the greatest density.

Although the cactus population is widespread, Darrell Ueckert at the Texas Agricultural Experiment Station in San Angelo says prickly pears do not appear to be extending their range. He is quick to add, however, that they are increasing in density in areas where they already exist.

Twenty-five and a half million acres of cactus produce a lot of fruit, and the tunas are probably more popular for human gourmandizing than *nopalitos*. Ripening in August and September, tunas can be peeled, cut up, sugared, and eaten like berries, with or without cream. They can even be made into pie. The juice can be cooked out of the tunas and used to make wine or jelly, or in combination with the pulp to make jam or marmalade.

Never try to handle the fruit barehanded or even with gloves. Gloves soon become loaded with glochids, which work through to your hands. Take along a pair of kitchen tongs. And pick only the dark purple tunas; these are fully ripe and will be filled with juice.

Yucca

JACK LOWRY

In the distance you see them rising against a mountain backdrop, their white plumes blowing in the wind. Around Easter time in West Texas, yucca blooms burst forth, dotting the grassy landscape with creamy flowers. Up close, the delicate spires of blossoms look like clusters of bells ready to ring in another Hudspeth County spring.

It's easy to confuse yuccas with sotol and agave, but a good handbook will help you tell them apart. Even Swiss botanist Jean Louis Berlandier, who came to Texas in the 1820s, frequently mistook yuccas for palm trees. Because there are so many yucca varieties, amateurs find it difficult to tell them apart.

Yuccas, like the sotols but unlike the agaves, are members of the lily family. They bloom every year, not once at the end of their lifetimes like the agave. So yuccas let you enjoy nature's springtime spectacle again and again.

When you visit an area like Hudspeth County today, feast your eyes on the attractive stands of the hardy yucca, but remember, yuccas once were a matter of life or death to early settlers who had to rely on plants for their survival.

Soon after Indians came to the region that is now West Texas some twelve thousand years ago, they began to use yuccas as they did so many other desert plants. They ate the buds, flowers, fruits, and stalks. Various parts of the plant would be boiled, roasted, ground into meal, or eaten raw.

Indians discovered that they could use the dried leaves to fashion footwear and weave baskets. They could twist the tough fibers to make ropes, weave them into mats, or cut and bind them together to make brushes. In a pinch, they could even use the sharp spines on the tips of the leaves to pierce the skin and relieve a poisonous snake bite.

Millennia after the Indians arrived in Texas, Spanish, Mexican, and American settlers also learned the uses of desert plants. They shaped the woody yucca stalks and stems into tools for hunting or digging, and from the hard points at the end of the blades they made a passable awl. They used clusters of the leaves to thatch roofs, and leaf blades with the needle point attached could be used to hold down the thatching.

They might break the leaf at the sharp point on the tip, peel it back, and *voila!* they had needle and thread in one long strand to mend torn clothing.

Even today, rural Mexicans mix salves to treat wounds by combining crushed yucca leaves with goat or sheep tallow. And from the juice of the fruit they prepare fermented drinks.

Yuccas contain the toxic substance saponin, which some Mexicans and Indians use to make soap. If you remove the bark, the roots can be crushed in water to produce a soapy cleansing solution. That's why some varieties of yucca are called soapweed.

The late naturalist Euell Gibbons recalled that the Navajos used yucca shampoo, claiming that it had hair-restoring qualities. When asked

A yucca about to burst into bloom. The tough leaf fibers can be woven or used as a coarse thread.—Jack Lewis

Yucca plants may rise twenty feet or more, but are generally shorter.—Jack Lewis

whether the shampoo worked, the Indians replied, "Have you ever seen a bald Navajo?"

Yuccas grow bloomstalks that yield hundreds of flowers. Some mature varieties are said to grow stalks that weigh as much as sixty or seventy pounds.

Early settlers supplemented their diet with the flowers and fruits of a variety of yuccas. Modern-day aficionados claim that the flowers add a hint of floral sweetness to salads.

The bloomstalks can be bitter, but the fruits of several of the Texas yuccas are popular eaten raw, roasted, or baked. Depending on how you prepare them, their flavor has been likened to either squash or Brussels sprouts. Nevertheless, in *Journey to Mexico during the Years 1826 to 1834,* Berlandier describes the fruit as "sweet but not very agreeable . . . somewhat analogous to that of the gum tree."

Yucca flowers contain a sticky pollen and reproductive organs that are remote from each other, properties that make self-pollination unlikely. For yuccas to reproduce, pollen must be carried by an outside agent.

That's where a tiny moth comes into the picture. The powdery white yucca moth enters newly opened flowers and collects a mass of pollen that she tucks in a receptacle behind her head. She lays an egg on the flower ovary, then fertilizes the plant by forcing the pollen inside the cavity where the pollen-receptive stigmas lie. She repeats the action on flower after flower and yucca after yucca.

El Capitan peak and the Guadalupe Mountains rise as a backdrop to yuccas in West Texas. Yuccas add new growth at the top and let their dead leaves fall around them like a grass skirt.—Jack Lewis

The moth hatchlings develop inside the fruit and feed on the nutritious yucca seeds. Eventually the larvae chew through the fruit and drop to the ground, where they burrow into the soil to continue their development. When the yuccas bloom the following year, the young yucca moths emerge to perpetuate this classic symbiotic drama.

While yuccas are usually associated with dry western landscapes, a species with a fountain-like growth, Y. louisianansis, grows wild in the Big Thicket and a few other parts of East Texas.

The Marvelous Maligned Mesquite

KEITH ELLIOTT

In faraway places there suddenly flourishes a mesquite mania. What Texans have known for generations—that the sweet smoke of smoldering mesquite wood lends uncommon savor to grilled meats—has been discovered out yonder, beyond Texas.

Restaurants in New York and Philadelphia, Cleveland and Minneapolis, even London and Paris are searing steaks—and fowl and seafood—over glowing coals of mystic mesquite. Clearly, yum's the word for mesquite cookery nowadays, and high time. The humble mesquite may be the most maligned, and most misunderstood, tree in the memory of man, notwithstanding the one of Good and Evil. Depending on point of view, the mesquite in Texas is perceived as bane or boon. Its stubborn presence among us is at the least a thorny issue.

On the one hand, there is W. T. Waggoner, pioneer rancher of northwest Texas. He scorned the mesquite as being "the devil with roots. It scabs my cows, spooks my horses, and gives little shade." Still, he admitted forlornly, "It gives the only shade there is, just about."

On the other hand there is J. Frank Dobie, bard of South Texas. He exulted: "No day can be counted entirely lost which begins with the smell of a mesquite fire at dawn and the taste of coffee boiled over it."

Old-timers speak of an era in earlier Texas when there were far fewer mesquite trees than today. They, along with some historians and naturalists, believe that the mesquite originated in Mexico. It made its way to the American Southwest, the theory goes, when its seeds were distributed in the excrement of burros, horses, and migratory birds. The hitchhiking, thorn-borne seedpods also broadcast themselves as they rode such creatures and the wind, it is believed.

Well, yes and no, according to Del Weniger, biology professor at Our Lady of the Lake University in San Antonio. He reports that early explorers and surveyors made more than ten thousand references to mesquite trees in widespread parts of Texas between about 1660 and 1860. Thus, Weniger believes, "the mesquite is quite as native to Texas as it is to Mexico. It was abundant throughout western Texas long before the appearance of domestic livestock on the scene."

Weniger's research suggests that mesquite trees flourished in reaches comprising 140 present-day Texas counties in the two centuries before 1860. Captain John Popek, he says, surveyed parts of Texas for a projected western railroad in 1854 and reported forests of mesquite trees that were thirty feet high and four to ten inches in diameter. Railway management need never worry about fuel

A mesquite tree stands as a storm passes. —Wyman Meinzer, Texas Parks & Wildlife Magazine

Mesquite adapts to varied conditions in over sixty million acres of the Southwest. Tough and hardy, it has resisted all efforts to eradicate it.—Wyman Meinzer, Texas Parks & Wildlife *Magazine*

for its woodburning locomotives, Popek declared, or fret about material for railroad ties.

But such abundance was sadly short-lived, according to Weniger. After the Civil War, during the stirring days of the Longhorn drives and the infancy of the Texas cattle industry, millions of prairie acres were denuded of their *mesquitals*—places where mesquite abounds. "Vast acreages of mesquite were practically eliminated in the Nu-

eces River valley in the 1870s, for example. I read of a single ranch with a fence made of mesquite trunks six feet high, touching each other, that stretched for fifteen miles."

So old-timers who recall Texas as being largely void of mesquite at the turn of the century are entirely correct, he believes. "Trees were burned, grubbed out, and chopped down for use as fuel, lumber, and fence posts. Mesquite makes good fence posts, because it is slow to rot. It's durable, too—some of the pioneers called it 'Texas ironwood.' Did you know that downtown Houston Street here in San Antonio was once paved with mesquite blocks? Bumpy, I suppose, but tougher than concrete."

Mesquite paving blocks lined the streets of turn-of-the-century Brownsville, too. Pioneers used mesquite for the hubs and spokes of wagon wheels and for the ribs and knees of boats. Furniture for the headquarters of the famed King Ranch is made of mesquite. Mesquite was used as timbering in the original Alamo built in 1718. And a cannon fired in Mexico's war against Spain for independence was fashioned by the patriot José Maria Morelos from a hollowed mesquite log. It may be viewed today in Mexico City's National Museum.

Hardly more than a bush on the far western plains of Texas, the mesquite is often a regal tree in the state's wetter reaches, especially along tributary bottoms. The national champion mesquite, in Real County, has a trunk twelve feet, eight inches in circumference, and its branches form an umbrella fifty-two feet high and seventy-one feet wide.

Many Texans believe the mesquite to be more reliable as a harbinger of spring than the robin or the groundhog. "Plant cotton when the mesquite tree leafs" is an ancient folk saying, and a wise one. When the mesquite buds, there is no longer threat of frost—that is the rural gospel. Warning, though: Trust only the older mesquites. The youngsters may rush the season and try on their finery before the party begins.

In some ways, the mesquite is not an easy tree to love. It is a defiant growth with cruel thorns and impenetrable brush, a come-and-take-it kind of tree. Little wonder that Sunday ranchers bulldoze, root-plow, burn, and grub it from their pastures.

Dr. Peter Felker of Texas A&I University, at Kingsville, disdains the popular view that mesquite depletes precious water. It drinks no more than other trees, he says. "I don't see mesquite as most people see mesquite," he admits. "I see mesquite as a nitrogen-fixing tree, capable of dealing with a lot of drought and capable of enriching the soil. Capable, too, of providing beans that have been a major food source of the Indians of the desert regions before the white men came, and a viable resource for animals."

Pioneers of the Texas Republic had a saying: "With prickly pear cactus apples alone, one can live, but with pear apples and mesquite beans, one will get fat." The mesquite has been a wondrous apothecary over the years. Nearly five hundred years ago, the Aztecs, who named the tree the *mizquitl*, ground its leaves to a powder, added water, and used the mixture to heal sore eyes. In rural Mexico, *curanderos* still use the ancient remedy.

Comanches chewed mesquite leaves to cure toothache. Yumas treated venereal disease with the leaves. Yaquis pulped them with water and urine to make a poultice for headaches. Mexican women boiled them with clothes as a bleach. Papagos used the mesquite's inner bark to ease indigestion. Various tribes have used the mesquite's gum, a sweetish amber substance, as a balm for wounds and sores, to mend pottery, to make black dye, to aid digestion, to brew into a tea for diarrhea, or simply to chew for pleasure. (Old-timers still chew mesquite gum in the belief it strengthens their hearts.)

Authorities say Texas contains about fifty million of the seventy million U.S. acres where mesquites are the dominant vegetation. The tree's haphazard and convoluted postures in the wild may seem grotesque to the formalist, but they are gaining favor among artists and artisans. Philip John Evett, native Englishman who is a sculptor and teacher of sculpture in San Antonio, is one of these. He believes mesquite is the most workable of woods for one of his calling. "It is more durable than mahogany," he says, "and its grains are lovely and unpredictable."

Jim Lee, a world-class woodturner from Reagan Wells in the Texas Hill Country, says simply, "Mesquite is the king of woods." Not a bad commentary on the most slandered tree of the Texas plains.

Spring Color in Texas

Spring in Central Texas is justly famous. Blankets of blue and red cover hillsides and valleys as bluebonnet, gaillardia, and Indian paintbrush burst into flower. Gradually the reds and blues of early spring give way to the pinks and whites of primrose and daisies, then to the vibrant yellows of coreopsis and brown-eyed susans appearing in summer. A thousand other wild-flowers of a thousand hues crowd into these vistas.

But this succession of shades is not limited to Central Texas. North and south, the state's roadsides and fields blaze with color. In the west, cactus blooms and prickly pear blossoms. The bluebonnet thrives there, too, in a taller

A mixed bouquet of wildflowers fills a spring field.—Bill Reaves

species with deeper, purplish tones. In the Big Thicket wild orchids and woods-loving flowers tint the scenery, and throughout East Texas the more subtle hues of wild azalea and dogwood herald springtime.

All around Texas, spring color delights anyone with an eye to see.

Wild azalea brightens the East Texas woods in early spring.—J. Griffis Smith →

The grandeur of spring at Big Bend National Park shows in the contrast of the brilliant red claret-cup cactus (Echinocereus triglochidiatus) and the stark Chisos Mountains, seen here at sunrise. —Tom Algire →

Western paintbrushes (Castilleja late-bracteata) nestled among bluebonnets. —David Muench

Spring Color 109

Fall Color in Texas

JACK LOWRY

Autumn winds blow multicolored leaves into springs of the Piney Woods. Changing patterns emerge as the leaves float on the surface.—Chester B. Robinson

Golden Days in East Texas

A cool autumn breeze sends wisps of smoke curling from the East Texas campfire. Red and gold leaves of sumac and sweetgum shimmer in the autumn sun. A stillness fills the woodlands. Along sylvan pathways, many-hued leaves and filtered patches of light create patterns. Rose, brown, and cream colored mushrooms spring from the forest floor.

In moist areas, cardinal flowers bloom. Although pines and palmettos are still summer green, dogwoods now display their scarlet berries and ruddy leaves. Before the first frost, birds feed on the few remaining reddish purple French mulberries.

But autumn in East Texas is more than a rich visual tapestry. Pause and listen. Nearby, you hear faint rustling and the crackle of dry leaves. A nine-banded armadillo rummages through the undergrowth. A squirrel scurries to collect nuts for winter. The tan, black, and brown patterns on the backs of timber rattlers create a perfect camouflage among the fallen leaves.

Tribes of Caddo Indians once roamed through these woods, where they cleared patches for their farms. Their bountiful harvests resulted in celebrations in the fall. From the forest floor they gathered hickory nuts, walnuts, and chinquapins by the basketful. With strong bows of Osage orange they hunted deer and bears. Years later, settlers from the north and east hunted hogs and squirrels here. In autumn they traded the Indians beef and pork for corn, nuts, deerskins, and venison.

In the twilight of the year, the days grow shorter and a chill fills the air. Winter fast approaches. Gusting from over the horizon, a crisp wind begins to shake the brittle leaves from beech trees and red oaks. Overhead, a flock of honking snow geese wings southward.

With shorter days and less sunlight, leaves stop producing chlorophyll, and that process leads to fall color in deciduous trees, shrubs, and vines.

Certain pigments in leaves are hidden by the strong green of the chlorophyll and become visible only as chlorophyll production slows down. Pigments such as carotene and xanthophyll produce oranges and yellows.

Because photosynthesis ceases with the absence of chlorophyll, greater amounts of sugar become trapped in the leaves. Trapped sugar causes anthocyanins to form, and these produce scarlet and purple colorations.

Weather influences the richness of pigmentation, so each season is different. Strong coloration depends on a good summer growing season, a dry autumn, and cool nights.

East Texas fall color usually peaks from late October through late November.

Scarlet and Gold in West Texas

When wintry gusts fill McKittrick Canyon late in October, the green leaves

Dashes of fiery red and harvest gold glow across placid waters of Daingerfield State Park.—J. Griffis Smith

of summer turn crimson and orange on walnut trees and big-tooth maples.

As the fall winds blow and the weeks pass, leaves tumble from the trees to carpet the ground with a colorful mosaic. By the middle of November, bare branches jut aloft, and the pools of McKittrick Creek rest silently, patterned in scarlet and gold.

Despite the power and stony majesty of its two-thousand-foot walls, McKittrick Canyon shelters a wide assortment of delicate ecosystems. This botanical and zoological oasis at the edge of the Chihuahuan Desert lures naturalists who read millions of years

of the earth's history on the canyon walls.

The exposed areas of the Capitan Reef can be seen in the Guadalupes, the Apache Mountains east of Van Horn, and the Glass Mountains east of Alpine. The 1,900-foot-high north wall of McKittrick Canyon gives a superb display of reef formations.

A small stream flows through the canyon, making the variety and abundance of vegetation possible. Visitors to West Texas are surprised to find Mc-Kittrick Creek tumbling down limestone boulders in the narrow channel it has carved out of the rock.

Forests seem incongruous in West Texas. Maples are more commonly found in temperate woods far to the north and east, and the Texas madrone reaches its northern limit here.—Jack Lewis →

Fall Color   113

Altitude, climate, springs, and the protected habitat allow rare species of plants to grow. The Texas madrone, more commonly found on the Sierra Madre of Mexico, reaches its northern limit here. You can easily identify the tree by its reddish wood and peculiar smooth light bark. The old bark scales off in layers. Madrone is also commonly called naked Indian and lady legs.

In madrone berry season (October and early November), raccoons and other animals gorge on the red fruit. But even in McKittrick, the endangered tree is declining. Deer and goats eat the sprouts and saplings, keeping new plants from maturing.

You're not likely to see bears in the canyon, although occasionally they make their way down from the high country. If you hear crashing steps, chances are you are listening to a mule deer. McKittrick Canyon may support as many as one hundred mule deer at a time.

As you walk along McKittrick Creek, you can hear gurgling eddies. In quiet pools, rainbow trout and sunfish dart among the rocks.

On cliffs high above the canyon, endangered peregrine falcons reportedly nest. Overhead, hawks soar. If you stand still, you might hear the whirring of hummingbirds feeding from cardinal flowers near the stream bed.

For more than ten thousand years, the springs, plants, wildlife, and mountain caves provided sustenance and a home to Indians. Spanish conquistadors who skirted the Guadalupes on their travels from Mexico in the late 1500s found nomadic Apaches inhabiting the area.

As you walk through the canyon in the fall, the brilliant leaves and blue sky accent the natural wonders that lured rugged souls here. The canyon, its wildlife and vegetation, remain a national treasure.

McKittrick Creek gives life to a canyon in Guadalupe Mountains National Park. —Tom Algire

Authors and Photographers

Formerly herbarium botanist at Texas A&M University, GEYATA AJILVSGI is now a freelance writer/photographer at work on two books on butterflies. She lives in Wimberley, Texas.

TOM ALGIRE is a freelance photographer who contributes to national magazines from his base in Merrill, Wisconsin.

STEVE ALVAREZ is a seventh-grade social studies teacher and a seasonal ranger for the National Park Service. He calls Garden City, Kansas, home.

At age forty-eight, FRANK BEESLEY took early retirement to work on a college education. He is now progressing on a doctorate at the University of Nebraska.

STEVE BENTSEN is a veterinarian in McAllen, Texas, who has twenty thousand heavily edited slides, many of them in his photographic specialty—wildlife in South Texas and Kenya.

JIM BONES of Tesuque, New Mexico, is a much-honored and oft-published photographer of wild places in the highest tradition of large view–camera, dye-transfer art.

KEITH ELLIOTT has written for *Reader's Digest*, *People*, and other top-flight magazines as well as *Texas Highways*. He calls both Houston and Austin home.

ANNE GARNER of Woodville was a teacher of high school English for fifteen years before setting her sights on a freelance writing career.

BOB GATES was a staff photographer with the Texas Department of Highways and Public Transportation until 1988, when he took another position with the department near Austin.

Freelancer HARRY GORDON of Boerne is primarily a motion-picture photographer but shoots stills when the occasion demands. He is a native of Michigan and studied his art in California.

RANDY GREEN, for years a mainstay of the *Texas Highways* staff, as his work in this book attests, is now a freelancer in Austin.

BARBARA HINTON, now president of the Orange Show, one of the country's finest exhibit institutions of environmental folk art, has lived in Houston since 1973.

LARRY HODGE, a former high school history teacher, is now a freelance writer and photographer living in Mason, in the Hill Country of Central Texas.

IRA KENNEDY of Austin is a fourth-generation Texan of Cherokee-Irish descent. His work on Enchanted Rock was published in *Sacred Sites*, a book on mystical landmarks in North America.

Texas Highways staffer JACK LEWIS is one of the masters of photographing the Texas scene. Museums as well as magazines pay tribute to his achievements.

Volunteer environmentalist JOE LIGGIO of Houston travels the Western Hemisphere for unusual nature photographs and finds the Big Thicket an inexhaustible resource.

FRANK LIVELY has been editor of *Texas Highways* since 1961, when it was a house organ for the Texas Department of Highways and Public Transportation. Now it ranks among the top state travel magazines, with national circulation.

JACK LOWRY, managing editor of *Texas Highways*, holds three college degrees and has been a newspaper editor and foreign correspondent. He began his career with the magazine in 1984.

WYMAN MEINZER of Benjamin has been freelancing for ten years and consistently has work published in major Texas and national publications, including *Audubon* and *National Wildlife*.

GLEN MILLS has been a still photographer for *Texas Parks & Wildlife* magazine for thirteen years. Earlier he worked in cinematography and television.

A determined champion of the land—and wilderness in particular—DAVID MUENCH specializes in recording photographically the "Spirit of Place." For twenty years a freelancer, he lives in Santa Barbara, California.

BOB PARVIN was a staff photographer for *Texas Highways* for several years before becoming a freelancer in 1981. He lives in Austin and photographs nature subjects throughout the state.

HOWARD PEACOCK, author of an award-winning book on the Big Thicket, free-lances and conducts writing workshops from his base in Woodville.

BILL REAVES is photography editor of *Texas Highways* magazine. He joined the staff in 1985, having worked nearly fifteen years with the Texas Parks and Wildlife Department.

RICHARD REYNOLDS is staff photographer for the Tourism Division of the Texas Department of Commerce. He makes his home in Austin.

CHESTER B. ROBINSON of Winnsboro is a third-generation photographer. He has exhibited his work in international photographic salons.

After several years as a photographer with Texas A&M University, J. GRIFFIS SMITH went to work on the staff of *Texas Highways* in 1984.

TRACY OWENS TORMA was a newspaper reporter in Longview and Marshall before establishing a freelance career in Houston. She specializes in corporate publications.

JOHN TVETEN has led Smithsonian Institution tours to many parts of the globe, from Cape Horn to the Grand Canyon. His articles and photographs have appeared in some fifty books and magazines.

ROSEMARY WILLIAMS became senior editor of *Texas Highways* in 1986, having been a writer and editor for the Department of Highways and Public Transportation since the early 1970s.

Index

The Nature of Texas was composed into type on a Compugraphic digital phototypesetter in ten and one-half point Goudy with three and one-half points of spacing between the lines. Goudy was also selected for display. The book was designed by Jim Billingsley, typeset by Metricomp, Inc., printed offset by Hart Graphics, Inc., and bound by John H. Dekker & Sons. The paper on which the book is printed is designed for an effective life of at least three hundred years.

Texas A&M University Press
College Station